Arthur Goddard

Players of the Period

First Series

Arthur Goddard

Players of the Period
First Series

ISBN/EAN: 9783337015374

Printed in Europe, USA, Canada, Australia, Japan

Cover: Foto ©ninafisch / pixelio.de

More available books at **www.hansebooks.com**

PLAYERS OF THE PERIOD.

A SERIES OF ANECDOTAL, BIOGRAPHICAL, AND CRITICAL MONOGRAPHS OF THE LEADING ENGLISH ACTORS OF THE DAY.

BY

ARTHUR GODDARD,

With Numerous Illustrations

BY

"ALMA," FRED. BARNARD, ALFRED BRYAN, PHIL MAY,
J. BERNARD PARTRIDGE, GEORGES PILOTELLE,
F. H. TOWNSEND, ETC.,

PHOTOGRAPHS OF THE SUBJECTS AND AUTOGRAPH QUOTATIONS.

FIRST SERIES.

LONDON: DEAN & SON, 160A, FLEET STREET.
1891.

PREFATORY NOTE.

NO attempt has been made in this volume to give a quite complete record of the careers and impersonations of the " Players of the Period" with whom it deals. Such an undertaking would be beyond the scope and foreign to the purpose of the work, the aim of which is rather, by the aid of reminiscences of popular actors in their principal parts, supplemented by personal and professional anecdotes and biographical notes, portraits, and character-sketches, to depict by pen and pencil representative players in the rôles with which they are most widely identified, and so stimulate the memories of playgoers, and call up in their minds countless recollections of pleasant hours owed to the arts of the actor and the dramatist, and to the glamour of the modern stage, which, by perfection of mechanical and artistic realism and illusion, imports an element of romance and poetry into the prose of life, and compels us to rank the theatre as the most popular intellectual pleasure of the period.

Considerations of space have made it impossible to include in this volume many admirable actors whose talent would have assured them a place in any such work had it not been deemed advisable to select subjects not only for their ability, but as representing distinct schools of acting; and a supplementary volume is in preparation, in which many players now unavoidably omitted will be represented.

My cordial thanks are due to Mr. Alfred Gibbons for his kind permission to reproduce a number of the admirable character-sketches which originally appeared in the pages of the "Lady's Pictorial;" to Mr. W. J. Ingram for similar permission in regard to the illustration by Mr. Bernard Partridge of Mr. Henry Irving as "Mephistopheles," which originally appeared in the "Illustrated London News;" and to Mr. Henry Irving for permission to reproduce certain illustrations from the Lyceum Souvenirs of "Macbeth" and "The Dead Heart."

ARTHUR GODDARD.

CONTENTS.

HENRY IRVING.

PAGE

An Ugly Duckling—First Appearance—An Odd Attraction—Diderot's Theory—Oscar Wilde—The David of the Drama—Slaying the Philistine—At Home—Prehistrionic Times—Garrick and George II.—What the Stage Does — Contrasts and Chasms — University Honours—London Début—An Odd Badge—*The Bells* —Irvingmania and Irvingphobia—Charles I.—The Psychology of Crime—A Prince of the Church— Actors' Mannerisms—The Chinese Ambassador—A Clashing of Critics—The Actor and the Poet Laureate —A Study of Malignant Senility—An Excellent Ideal —Engagement of Miss Ellen Terry—An Unconventional Shylock—*The Corsican Brothers*—A Sensual Pagan—Romeo and Benedick—A Unique Banquet —A Farewell Demonstration—Compliments and Canvas-back Ducks—" Fussie "—Malvolio—A Curiosity of Criticism—Mr. William Winter's Poetical Address— Diplomacy—Goldsmith's Ideal—Goethe Anglicised

—A Perfect Mephistopheles—*Werner*—Exploiting a
Revolution—*Ravenswood* 17

WILSON BARRETT.

First Appearance—A Doubtful Pie—Romantic Heroes
—A Wasted Play—Life as it is—Zolaistic Naturalism
—*The Silver King*—The "Spider's Whistle"—A
Touching Story—*Claudian—Chatterton*—A Comprehensible Hamlet—A Queer Experience—*Junius*
—The Passions in Arcadia—A Village Othello—
A Gallant Cavalier—*Clito*—The Ideal Woman—A
Muscular Christian—Dan Mylrea—Plain John Saxton
—*The People's Idol*—The Actor at Home . . . 117

H. BEERBOHM TREE.

The Chameleon of the Stage—The Ideal Actor—A Caged
Lion—An Irishman's Advice—Sir Andrew Aguecheek
—Qualifications, Real and Imaginary—" Something
Wrong in his Inside"—A Polished Rascal—A
Gallery of Scoundrels—*The Private Secretary*—Sir
Mervyn Ferrand—A Libel on Humanity—A Railway
Metamorphosis—Paul Demetrius—The Actor-Manager's Controversy—Our Mother-in-law, The County
Council—A Revolutionary Poet—Humanity at its
Best—A Fascinating Bushranger—A Study in Monomania—A Gloating Falstaff—*A Man's Shadow*—
Laroque and Luversan—A Soul-torn Priest—*Beau*

Austin—A Sublimated Horatio Sparkins—Vice, Virtue, and Versatility—A Duke and a Dancing Girl 185

E. S. WILLARD.

A Society Villain — "Responsible Utility"— Dramatic Method—At Home—A Tender Dramatic Conscience —First London Chance—"The Spider"—The New Villain—A Terrible Curse—A Natural Claudius—A Splendid Sinner—Hard Middle-age—A Greek Voluptuary and a Roundhead Rascal—"The Tiger"— Macbeth — *The Monk's Room* — Cyrus Blenkarn— Capital and Labour—"*I* Buy Now!"—An *Al Fresco* Understudy — Filippo — Judah Llewellyn — Judah's Sole Virtue—A Converted Deacon—In Shakespeare's Inn—In America 241

S. B. BANCROFT.

The Sublimation of the Swell—Typical Men about Town—Complete Man, Perfect Gentleman—A Stage-stricken Youth—The First Robertsonian Comedy— A New Stage Fop—An Impudent Adventurer—Jack Poyntz—Triplet—A Broken-down Gentleman—*Diplomacy*—The *Scène des Trois Hommes*—Abolition of the Pit—Count Loris Ipanoff—*Lords and Commons*—The Farewell Night—*The Dead Heart*—The Actor off the Stage—Arbitration—A Word Duel . 297

JOHN LAWRENCE TOOLE.

PAGE

In 1838—Civic Sweetness and Light—Toole and Cruikshank—The *Piano* Pedal of Pathos—A Nineteenth-Century Yorick—Practical Jokes—First Appearance—John Lavers—Mr. Spriggins—Caleb Plummer—The Phonographic Epilogue—Michael Garner—Highways and Byeways—A Good Heart—The Comedian at Home—Dick Dolland—How a "Wheeze" was Obtained—Paul Pry—The 1874 Banquet—Lord Rosebery's Unconscious Prophecy—"Bolo"—Toole's Theatre—Mr. Barnaby Doublechick—"The Speaker's Eye"—"Paw Clawdian"—From Butler to Oxford Don—A Breakfast with Mr. Gladstone—The Australian Project—Dining with the Prince of Wales—"God-speed" 337

LIST OF ILLUSTRATIONS.

Portrait of MR. HENRY IRVING . . *Frontispiece.*

PAGE

Mr. Irving as "Charles I." . . By *Horace Morehen* . 37
,, ,, "Hamlet" . . . ,, ,, ,, . 41
,, ,, ,, "Shylock" . . ,, ,, ,, . 60
,, ,, "Benedick" . ,, ,, ,, . 68
,, ,, "Malvolio" . . ,, ,, ,, . 79
,, ,, "Mephistopheles" . ,, *J. Bernard Partridge* 89
,, ,, "Robert Macaire," and
Mr. Weedon Grossmith
as "Jacques Strop" . By *F. H. Townsend* . 99
,, ,, "Macbeth" . . ,, *J. Bernard Partridge* 101
,, ,, "Robert Landry" . ,, ,, ,, 105
,, ,, "Ravenswood" 109
Portrait of MR. WILSON BARRETT 116
Mr. Wilson Barrett as "Hamlet" . By *T. H. Wilson* . 139
,, ,, ,, "Jack Yeulett" ,, *J. Bernard Partridge* 159
,, ,, ,, "Lord Harry
Bendish" . ,, ,, ,, 163
Portrait of MR. H. BEERBOHM TREE. 184
Mr. Tree as "Prince Borowski" After *J. Bernard Partridge* 197

LIST OF ILLUSTRATIONS.

PAGE

Mr. Tree as "Sir Mervyn Ferrand"   After *J. Bernard Partridge* 205
,,   ,,   "Falstaff" . . . By *Alfred Bryan* . . 225

Portrait of MR. E. S. WILLARD 240
Mr. Willard as "The Spider" . After *J. Bernard Partridge* 255
,,   ,,   "Mark Lezzard" . By   ,,   ,,   265
,,   ,,   "Captain Ezra Promise",,   ,,   ,,   267

Portrait of MR. S. B. BANCROFT. 296
Mr. Bancroft as "Jack Poyntz" . By *Horace Morehen* . 313
,,   ,,   "Triplet" . . . ,,   ,,   ,,   . 317
,,   ,,   "Count Orloff". . ,,   ,,   ,,   . 321

Portrait of MR. J. L. TOOLE 336
Mr. Toole and the *gamins* . . . By *Alfred Bryan* . . 344
,,   ,, as "Caleb Plummer". . ,, *Fred. Barnard* . . 347
,,   ,,   "Paul Pry" . . . ,, *Alfred Bryan* . . 357

PLAYERS OF THE PERIOD.

HENRY IRVING.

THERE was once an ugly duckling, and many of the other ducklings, and of the ducks too, for that matter, except just a few who saw a little further than the end of their bills, were disposed to jeer at it, because it declined to turn its toes out like a conventional, well-brought-up duck. And some critical turkey-cocks, invested with spurs, and therefore thinking themselves emperors, blew themselves out like ships in full sail and bore straight down upon it, gobbled, and grew quite red in the face. But, despite many troubles, the ugly duckling, braving the quackings and the peckings, took the water and saw its own image, only to find itself—a swan. And after a time he heard them all saying that he was the most beautiful of all the birds. Even the turkey-cocks moderated their rancour, and the sun of popular favour shone warm and bright. And the name of the ugly duckling was Henry Irving.

Thirty years ago just one or two shrewd readers of men, such as Charles Dickens—who had been much impressed by Mr. Irving's acting in *Uncle Dick's Darling*, remarking, "That young man will be a great actor"—and Adelaide Kemble, recognised the coming actor in the fluttering, frightened *débutant*, who, on his first appearance on the stage of the New Royal Lyceum Theatre, Sunderland, on September 29th, 1856, when the play was *Richelieu*, and the young actor had to utter the first words spoken in the play, "Here's to our enterprise!" was a dire failure; and on his second, as Cleomenes in *A Winter's Tale*, incontinently took to his heels, covering his retreat with a gasping, incoherent adjuration to his fellow-actors to "come on to the market-place." Yet, in this timid, stage-frightened Cleomenes was to be found, in the fulness of time, the populariser of Shakespeare, the brilliant and scholarly exponent of Shakespearean creations, the most intellectually and æsthetically satisfying Hamlet, Shylock, Benedick, of the modern stage; a Romeo who should be a veritable type of the triumph of mind over body; a Macbeth who, while original and occasionally antipathetic, should yet compel respect as a thoughtful and scholarly psychological study.

That Mr. Irving's *début* in the North should have not been an instantaneous triumph is not surprising when the taste of local audiences at that period is taken into account. Even as recently as 1880 an action was brought against a manager at Barnsley, to restrict him from producing a drama which excited the enthusiasm of the audience to such a pitch that it became a nuisance, the play in question being *The Six Stages of Crime; or, Wine, Women, Gambling, Theft, Murder, and the Gallows,*—an additional attraction being the son of Charles Peace, the burglar-murderer, who played the concertina and answered any questions put to him by the audience.

The record of an actor who has appeared in more than six hundred and fifty parts is terrifying to a conscientious chronicler, and compels an eclecticism that under other conditions might seem unreasonably narrow. But the only possible method of dealing with such a career with the hope of giving a just idea of the artistic nature and capacity of the actor, is to indicate the impersonations in which he has achieved the greatest distinction, and which have also served to illustrate most lucidly the opulence of his resources.

An actor who has succeeded in satisfying a cultured and critical section of the playgoing public in characters so numerous and diverse that nothing less than an Irving Encyclopædia could deal exhaustively with his *répertoire*, is a living negation of Got's cynical axiom that a great actor should have no brains beyond those essential to a mere mimic. He offers, also, in his own person, an argument in qualified support of Diderot's theory that an actor should have no sensibility. For it is clear that while Mr. Irving has won and kept his position by sheer brain-power, it is impossible that he can have felt in his own person all the storm and stress of passion, all the heartbreaking pathos, all the brain-sucking cynicism of the dramatic characters which he has represented, except within the limits which he himself has assigned, namely, that it is quite possible for an actor who has mastered his art to feel all the excitement of the situation and yet be perfectly self-possessed. Otherwise he must have been, long ere this, a wreck of over-wrought nerves, a hopeless hypochondriac, a melancholy ghost of manhood, instead of the brilliant, tactful, astute informing spirit of the Lyceum.

Upon this point there is something to be said for Mr. Oscar Wilde's theory : " We must go to Art for everything, because Art does not hurt us. The tears that we shed at a play are a type of the exquisite sterile emotions that it is the function of Art to awaken in us. We weep, but we are not wounded. We grieve, but our grief is not bitter. In the actual life of man, sorrow, as Spinoza says somewhere, is a passage to a lesser perfection, but the sorrow with which Art fills us both purifies and initiates. . . . Emotion for the sake of emotion is the aim of Art, and emotion for the sake of action is the aim of life."

Mr. Irving occupies a position in the social history of his period that is unique. He is not simply a great actor. There are even to-day those who deny him any claim to histrionic greatness, as they consider that his "mannerisms" handicap him too severely—as if every really strong man, whether in the dramatic or any of its sister arts, did not prove his strength by individuality of style, or, as the unbelievers prefer to dub it, "mannerism." But he is more than a celebrated actor. He is a distinguished figure in the social life of to-day, and, more than that, he is a living influence.

Henry Irving is the David of the drama. After the disappearance from the stage of Macready, in 1851, with the honourable exceptions of the efforts of Charles Kean at the Princess's Theatre and Samuel Phelps at the remote and therefore comparatively uninfluential Sadler's Wells, the stage had lapsed into a lamentably commonplace and conventional —not to say comatose—condition, varied with occasional visitations of nightmare. The Goliath of Philistinism strutted in self-satisfied complacency until this dramatic David came

from his provincial wanderings, and slew the
Philistine with the smooth stone of polished,
intellectual art.

With the advent of Irving, culture killed
conventionality and claptrap; intellectual distinction triumphed over commonplace dulness
and brain proved its superiority alike to the
banality of burlesque, the soulless splendour of
spectacle, and the mania and mouthings of
melodrama. Moreover, as regards the actor
himself, the subtle chemistry of intellect has
transmuted "mannerism" into personal distinction, and metamorphosed potential weakness
into added strength.

Mr. Irving's artistic feeling is innate, and
displays itself as unmistakably in his private
life as upon the stage. His chambers in
Grafton Street, so grim externally, and his
house at Hammersmith, are full of quaint and
interesting things,—beautiful old engravings of
great actors of the past, curiously carved old
cabinets, sketches of the actor himself in character, cabinets crowded with curious relics of
dead-and-gone players—rings, "properties" of
all sorts, and a host of interesting souvenirs

which Mr. Irving's admirers have taken occasion to present to him from time to time; books everywhere, on shelves, tables, chairs, the floor—an unfailing token of the great actor's student-nature, and many of them of great rarity and value; statuettes of Mephistopheles and Don Quixote, with charming Miss Ellen Terry as a foil to their grim picturesqueness; pictures of every kind, and each with some special charm of its own; dogs, including the prime favourite "Fussie;" and a thousand-and-one pleasant and graceful indications of the refined, artistic nature of the foremost player of the period.

Nor is the great actor himself less picturesque and delightful. The pink of courtesy and the prince of hosts, his high-bred manner and rich voice, his strongly-marked features, so full of character, and illumined by "twin stars, which nature has stuck in his head," as Colman said of Garrick, make up a personality full of charm and fascination.

Success has not spoiled Mr. Irving. He is to-day as unaffected, cordial, kindly, and hard-working as he was in the long-past period when "plain living" was the necessity, and "high thinking" the rule, of his life ; and he is to the full as popular as a man as he is as an actor. His heart is ever sympathetic, his ear ever willing to listen to the voice of the timid or the suffering, his head and hand ever ready to counsel and to aid.

It is an interesting speculation whether in the midst of his histrionic triumphs Mr. Irving's thoughts ever revert to that memorable morning when, leaving his humdrum duties in the quiet back office of Messrs. Thacker & Co., in Newgate Street, where for about three years the embryo tragedian had carried out with conscientious care the work of an invoice clerk, he paid a visit to Phelps at Crosby Hall, in Bishopsgate Street, and, encouraged by the great actor's opinion of his single recitation, took the step which proved the turning-point in his life, returned to his office, and then and there "gave notice" to his employers, and announced his intention of adopting the stage as a profession.

There are members of the staff of the well-known firm in Newgate Street who still retain pleasant memories of the gentlemanly and amiable young Henry Brodribb, who came to their office from school, displayed so much assiduity and care in his work, and was so keenly alive to the refinements of life as to institute among the clerks who shared his desk a little code of rules, by which each agreed to be subject to a small fine for any lapse from the niceties of grammar or any of the proprieties of speech.

From the first the young fellow was fond of poetry and of reciting, yet, had not the artistic temperament been so strong within him, the world of art would probably have never known a Henry Irving, but the world of commerce might have been the richer to-day by an Anglo-Indian Henry Brodribb, sedate, methodical, pursy perhaps, and liverless. That instead of this estimable but possibly rather prosaic person we have the brilliant actor-manager of the Lyceum, is a curious example of the truth of the axiom, " Talent does what it can : Genius does what it must ! "

It is not so many years since Watkins Burroughs, disgusted at the indifference of his patrons to the merits of the legitimate drama, festooned the doors of the Preston Theatre with crape, and painted over them the inscription :—

> **Gone into Mourning**
>
> FOR BRAINS, GOOD TASTE, AND APPRECIATION,
>
> DEFUNCT
>
> AMONGST THE UPPER TEN OF PRESTON.

Mr. Irving has done more than any other living actor to render a repetition of any such practical satire impossible, although there are still slow-witted people who can no more appreciate his delicate art than George II. could that of Garrick, of whom it is on record that, after seeing the great little actor in *Richard III.*, all that impressed the royal mind was the Lord Mayor; and Garrick, thirsting for criticism of Richard, was fain to content himself with the King's rhapsodical ejaculations : "I do love dat Lord Mayor. Capital Lord Mayor! Fine Lord Mayor, dat, Mr. Garrick ; where you get such capital Lord Mayor ?"

The provincial experience of Mr. Irving, naturally more or less of a probationary and educational phase in his career, may be dismissed with the truism that to the hard work and varied impersonations which it entailed London owes the present institution of the Lyceum Theatre. As Mr. Irving himself says, " The lucky actor works ; " and it is, without question, to incessant, conscientious work, in the study and on the stage, that he owes, to a great extent, the position which he now enjoys.

But still more do we owe the Lyceum drama of to-day to the actor-manager's worthy conception of the responsibilities and potentialities of the stage and of the actor's calling. Mr. Irving has said with truth : " To the thoughtful and reading man the stage brings the life, the fire, the colour, the vivid instinct which are beyond the reach of study. To the common, indifferent man, immersed as a rule in the business and socialities of daily life, it brings visions of glory and adventure, of emotion and of broad human interest. . . . To the most torpid and unobservant it exhibits the humorous in life, and the sparkle and *finesse* of language, which in dull ordinary existence are shut out of knowledge or omitted from particular notice. To all it uncurtains a world, not that in which they live, and yet not other than it—a world in which interest is heightened, and yet the conditions of truth are observed ; in which the capabilities of men and women are seen developed without losing their consistency to nature, and developed with a curious fidelity to simple and universal instincts of clear right and wrong."

Upon another occasion, and referring more particularly to the functions of the individual actor, Mr. Irving said : " Acting, like every other art, has a mechanism. No painter, however great his imaginative power, can succeed in pure ignorance of the technicalities of his art ; and no actor can make much progress till he has mastered a certain mechanism which is within the scope of patient intelligence. Beyond that is the sphere in which a magnetic personality exercises a power of sympathy which is irresistible and indefinable. That is great acting ; but though it is inborn, and cannot be taught, it can be brought forth only when the actor is master of the methods of his craft." Upon these two maxims, it may be said, hang all the laws of the higher drama.

And how has Mr. Irving translated his precepts into practice; crystallised his theories into actualities? To form a just estimate of this it is necessary to ignore to some extent the second stage of his professional evolution, when he was acting under the Bateman management—at all events until his insistence upon the dramatic possibilities of *The Bells*, which made the Bateman management successful, and gave him his first untrammelled opportunity of making a mark with metropolitan audiences —judging him rather by what he has done under the favourable, if onerous, conditions of being answerable only to himself and the public, and free to carry out in their integrity and to their ultimate power his individual theories and principles.

Of a truth Mr. Irving has not at any period let his critics languish for lack of material. The mere repetition of his principal impersonations is like the Homeric catalogue of ships. From the refined comedy of Benedick to the brutal blackguardism of Bill Sikes; from the pure, gentle, ideal spirituality and sweet humanity of the Vicar of Wakefield to the diabolical, mocking cynicism of Mephistopheles; from the dignity of Charles I. and the curiously pathetic passion of Shylock to the flippant rascality of Jingle and the airy insolence of Digby Grant; from the haunting terror of Mathias and the conscience-stricken misery of Eugene Aram to the subtle treachery of Iago and the airy comedy of Doricourt; from the vulpine cunning of Louis XI. and the wittier brilliancy of Richelieu to the vivid contrast of a Dubosc and Lesurques, the devil-may-care knavery of a Robert Macaire and the pathos and nobility of a Robert Landry, are huge physical and psychical chasms for the genius of one actor to bridge. It would also be unjust to deny that, despite the fact that the marked individualities of Mr. Irving's physique and method necessarily make each of these impersonations to a certain extent a variation of himself, yet each possesses a distinct identity, and, for the time at least, entirely satisfies the intellectual appetite of the audience.

Mr. Irving has upon three occasions had the honour of delivering an address by special invitation before the authorities and undergraduates, professors and students, of three Universities. The first occasion was on November 29th, 1876, when he was honoured by an address delivered to him, in the Dining Hall of Trinity College, Dublin, by the graduates and undergraduates, in the presence of the highest officers of the University, the address being read by the Member of Parliament for the University. On March 30th, 1885, at the invitation of the professors and students of Harvard University, Cambridge, U.S.A., Mr. Irving delivered a lecture on "Dramatic Art" at Sander's Theatre, Boston, before a crowded and enthusiastic audience, many members of which had come specially from New York. Mr. Irving gave then an eloquent exposition of his well-loved art, and combated the prejudicial impression many hold of a player's calling because he represents only feigned emotions, by pointing out that "this would apply with equal force to poet and novelist." After the address, President Eliot gave a reception to Mr. Irving, at which nearly all the Professors of Harvard University and the notables present in the theatre attended. The third occasion was on June 26th, 1886, at Oxford, when Mr. Irving delivered an address on "Four Great Actors," before the heads of the Colleges and a remarkable gathering of distinguished scholars.

It was in 1859, at the Princess's Theatre, that Mr. Irving made his first appearance upon the London stage, but, with sound discretion, failing to see an opportunity of substantial advancement, he relinquished his engagement, returned to the provinces, and only came back to the metropolis after some years of further apprenticeship, to take leading parts at the St. James's Theatre, under the management of Miss Herbert, where he appeared, on October 6th, 1866, as Doricourt, in *The Belle's Stratagem*, and at once proved himself a master of light and polished comedy.

Then followed a medley of impersonations including a revival of Rawdon Scudamore in *Hunted Down*, a character which Mr. Irving had created with striking success in the provinces; Harry Dornton in *The Road to Ruin;*

both Joseph and Charles Surface in *The School for Scandal;* Robert Macaire, Petruchio, Bob Gassit in *Dearer than Life;* a realistic Bill Sikes, a creation of genuine power and originality; Young Marlow in *She Stoops to Conquer;* John Peerybingle in *Dot*, in which Mr. Irving showed that he could depict homely pathos as effectively as the nonchalant gaiety of light comedy or the power and depth of tragedy; Reginald Chevenix in *Uncle Dick's Darling;* Digby Grant in *The Two Roses*, a finished study of gentlemanly rascaldom, full of originality and polished to the last degree; an admirably impudent Jingle in *Pickwick*—the oddest prelude conceivable to the creation which stimulated the fortunes of the Bateman management at the Lyceum, and compelled all the town to flock to see the newly-revealed dramatic comet which was glowing luridly in the weird, fantastic, thrilling character of Mathias in *The Bells*, that powerful melodrama, in which, like Single Speech Hamilton, poor one-play Leopold Lewis apparently exhausted his dramatic resources.

And here it may not be out of place to

correct a misapprehension which was, at all events at one time, prevalent, to the effect that while *The Bells* made Mr. Irving, he neglected to help poor Lewis in the days of his decline. Mr. Irving scrupulously regarded the *amour-propre* of the broken-down playwright, and did not parade his benevolence, but as a matter of common justice it should be recorded that Leopold Lewis received countless kindnesses from Mr. Irving in the troubles sequent to an unfortunate career, and, during the last years of his life, received a regular income from the actor.

It is not altogether surprising that there was a time when a section of the critical wisdom of the day could find no more fitting badge for Mr. Irving than that of a light-character-eccentric-comedian. He was still, to it, the ugly duckling. It could not quite understand him and his originality, in which it only saw an exaggeration of character-acting, while his marked individuality appeared mere wanton, purposeless eccentricity. Instead of welcoming the advent of an actor who aimed above all else at fidelity of representation, and this in the face of so strongly-marked a physique as to make versatility doubly difficult, the critics of this particular school seemed as if they would have welcomed a return to the classic but constrictive use of masks, rather than that their ideal of a particular character should not be rigidly maintained.

With true artistic insight, Mr. Irving recognised in *The Bells*, rejected though it had been with contumely and cynical amusement by many a managerial wiseacre, his opportunity. Not without hesitation, not without protest, was the play produced. Disaster was predicted with cheerful confidence, and the judicious grieved over what was considered a foregone failure. But what was the result? The vivid realism, the apparent spontaneity, the grim picturesqueness, and, above all, the obvious truth to nature of the Mathias compelled attention, insisted upon serious criticism, even when they did not command the unqualified admiration of those who refused to hear the voice of this new and uncanny charmer.

Never has Mr. Irving's own theory as to the power of an actor who combines the magnetic force of a strong personality with a mastery of the resources of his art been more amply justified. Never, too, has he more plainly illustrated Diderot's paradox than in his creation of the haunted, conscience-stricken burgomaster, for, of a surety, the agony of the terror-stricken Mathias, the struggles of the dual nature—the eternal Ormuzd and Ahriman of humanity—could only be realised by the vivid imagination of an artist; and the secret of their hold upon the audience was to be found in their direct appeal to fundamental emotions, common to all ages, climes, and classes, made by an actor who was all the while a perfect master of his methods. As Mr. Irving has himself said: " Every jealous man does not utter laments as pathetic and eloquent as Othello's, but these are none the less human because they are couched in splendid diction. They move the hearer because they are the utterance of a man's agony. . . . The whole soul of an actor may be engaged in Hamlet's revenge upon Claudius, but he need not on that account feel any desire to slay the excellent gentleman who enacts the King."

No doubt for a while the sheer horror of the new Lyceum drama drew the public with all the primitive and powerful fascination of crime. The awful death of Mathias, the enthralling dream scene, the romantic realism of the whole thing, gripped the imagination even of the slowest-witted, much as if some ghastly crime had been enacted in their midst and was being served up to them with *sauce piquante* by the skilled special correspondents of an enterprising Press. But this *succès de l'horreur*, morbid and undesirable, soon gave place to an honest appreciation of the combined force and *finesse* with which a great actor could lift a part from its melodramatic low-level origin into the healthier air of tragedy, in which the passions of the audience might be stirred, not unworthily.

The courage of Mr. Irving in choosing this play was all the more remarkable as a different version of *Le Juif Polonais* had been produced at another theatre with anything but success. But in the hands of Mr. Irving the easily vulgarised figure of Mathias became a finished study profoundly true and thought-compelling, exhibiting human nature under conditions as exceptional as they were, in their own way, fascinating. Intensity and intelligence made the English version of MM. Erckmann-Chatrian's *étude-dramatique* a truly absorbing study, instead of merely an appalling and repellent story of a crime and its punishment; and, on the morning of November 26th, 1871, Mr. Irving awoke, in Byronic fashion, to find himself famous.

It was not long before society split into two camps—the Irving-idolaters, and the Anti-Irvingites. The individualities of the actor in gait and pronunciation were stigmatised as ineradicable blots or hailed as affording a new and higher criterion of histrionic excellence; and, as the "mannerisms" of the French dramatist Marivaux necessitated the coining of a new word, *marivaudage*, so the cult of the new dramatic star soon gave us Irvingese, Irvingmania, and Irvingphobia, and Henry Irving became a universal dinner-table topic, as indispensable as the weather, and far more interesting. For this alone Mr. Irving deserves well of his age, for while amusing subjects are not always interesting, and interesting subjects rarely amusing, he and his art are many-sided enough to be both. It would not be easy to mention any person and place the sudden blotting out of whom or which would make so lamentable a gap in the social life of to-day as Mr. Irving and the Lyceum Theatre.

From the morbid, monomaniacal Mathias Mr. Irving passed at a bound to the other extreme of his art, and appeared on April 1st, 1872, as Jeremy Diddler in the old-fashioned farce, *Raising the Wind*. But this was only an instance of *reculer pour mieux sauter*, and his next essay proved to be one of his finest creations, namely, that of Charles I. in Mr. W. G. Wills's poetical drama of that name.

It was on September 28th of the same year that Mr. Irving gave to the stage his dignified and touching picture of the White King—a work of rare beauty, softened by countless tender touches, invested with royal dignity, and illumined by an innate spirituality which seemed to surround the picturesque personality of the King with the sanctity of martyrdom.

The ascetic features of the actor, humanised and made gentle by the soft dark eyes and the tender smile, and with an intellectual beauty to

MR. HENRY IRVING AS CHARLES I.

many people far more fascinating than the comely curves, pink and white perfection, and sleek shapeliness of the stage Adonis, harmonised well with the dramatist's conception of the First Charles ; and the picturesque dress, a faithful copy of Van Dyck, with the calmly regal bearing, combined to make one of the most finished and refined stage pictures of the period. The unstudied grace of gesture, the high-bred inflections of the voice,—all were admirable, and those who have witnessed the magnificent moment when the King, flinging back his cloak with a superb gesture, half of contempt, half of simple confidence in " the divinity that doth hedge a king," held his breast at the mercy of the rebels' pikes ; or that final scene upon the threshold of the scaffold, when women sobbed and men were strangely moved as the pathos culminated in the King's farewell to his wife and little children, will not easily forget the Charles I. of Henry Irving.

That the melancholy beauty of the latest stage-version of Charles was intensified at the expense of Cromwell, who was painted with an unsparing brush as a human monster unfamiliar to the more judicial pages of the historian, does not alter the fact that Mr. Irving's creation was one of exceptional dignity ; and its conscientious elaboration proved that he was uttering no idle words when he expressed the opinion that to have an ideal in art, and to strive through one's life to embody it, may be a passion to the actor as it may be to the poet.

But the day of absolute realisation of his ideals was not yet come to the now celebrated actor. That was to be when, swaying a dual sceptre Mr. Irving should lord it at the Lyceum six years later as actor-manager. But how full of excellent work those six years of the Bateman management were! Creation followed creation, success succeeded success.

In April 1873 Mr. Wills provided Mr. Irving with a part absolutely opposed at all points to that of Charles, yet one which was peculiarly adapted to the actor's physique and to his methods as manifested in Mathias. As Eugene Aram, another study in the psychology of crime was made by Mr. Irving, and, with all the intensity of his mental power, he gave the world a representation of terror, remorse, bravado, and despair which will not be soon forgotten, evanescent as the greatest triumphs and most moving effects of an actor's art must inevitably be. The defiance of the vulgar Houseman, the agony in the churchyard, the moment when with true artistic instinct Aram falls at the foot of a cross in the dumb misery of despair, the final confession and death, were details which stamped the impersonation as more than merely clever; and the play-going public looked forward with exceptional interest to Mr. Irving's creation of Richelieu in Lord Lytton's drama of that name, which was announced for September 27th, 1873.

Here, too, a complete triumph awaited the actor. To this day there are not wanting those who consider that the wily, worldly old Cardinal was, and is, the best of Mr. Irving's many impersonations. But this opinion was not universal, and there were those who found Richelieu disappointing, complaining that for three acts he was spiritless, and in the fourth delirious. Delirious or no, the audience accepted with instinctive justice, and without a dissentient voice, Mr. Irving's impersonation as a vivid, intellectual presentment of an exceptionally interesting figure.

Here again Mr. Irving's make-up was fault-

MR. IRVING AS HAMLET.

less, his picturesqueness unmarred by a single inconsistency, his bearing perfect in its versatility. Sarcasm and philosophy, fierce priestly denunciation—as when he all at once clothes himself in the sacerdotal dignity of a prince of the Church, and threatens the sacrilegious servants of the King with the awful curse of Rome—all seemed to spring spontaneously from Richelieu's lips; and thus to make the key-note of the drama tragic is surely a higher interpretation than that of Macready, who presented the Cardinal as something very like a comic character in the earlier scenes of the play. After Mr. Irving's Richelieu it would be as reasonable to expect an intelligent public to accept the old-time reading of Shylock, as a comic part, to be played by the low-comedian of the company in a red wig.

The dramatic version of Balzac's romantic story of the bricked-up lover, written by Mr. Hamilton Aïdé under the title of *Philip* and produced on the stage of the Lyceum on February 7th, 1874, gave Mr. Irving one more opportunity of depicting the misery of remorse, accentuated this time by the addition of jealousy.

Philip is a sombre young Spaniard, the victim of remorse for the supposed murder of his half-brother, and consumed with jealousy of his wife. It can easily be imagined what Mr. Irving would make of these two powerful passions, and his Philip was a distinctly interesting study, despite many improbabilities in the circumstances by which he was conditioned.

After an intervening revival of *The Bells*, intense interest centred in the Lyceum again in October, on the 31st of which month Mr. Irving appeared as Hamlet.

There have been so many Hamlets, good, bad, and indifferent, that it might almost have been supposed that even an impersonation by so interesting an actor as Mr. Irving might excite but a languid and conventionally courteous show of interest, and secure nothing more satisfactory than a *succès d'estime*. But to English audiences there seems to be a perennial charm about this wonderful play, and it obviously possesses a peculiar fascination for actors.

It was objected by some sticklers for consistency that Mr. Irving was too old to play the Prince of Denmark with effect, as he could not look the part. Others thought that his "mannerisms" would render anything but a caricature of Hamlet impossible—as though "mannerisms," or a powerful personality, were not inseparable from great acting. As an old dramatist once said: "No man has ever been a popular favourite in my time unless he was a pronounced mannerist. Charles Kemble was a silver-toned, sententious mannerist; Edmund Kean was a stuttering, spasmodic mannerist; Macready and Phelps always grim and growling over their bones; Charles Kean had a chronic cold in the head; Keeley was sleek and sleepy; Buckstone a chuckler; Compton funny as a funeral; Ben Webster always imperfect, and had a Somersetshire dialect; Mathews a Mephisto in kid gloves and patent leather boots; Ryder a roarer,"—and it is an open question whether the so-called "mannerisms" of Henry Irving have not helped rather than hindered his popularity, even if now and then they have obtruded themselves out of season to the detriment, in some degree, of his art.

But mannerisms or no mannerisms, Hamlet was a success. Thoughtful to the minutest detail, distinguished, refined, picturesque, intelligent and intelligible, the new Hamlet made his mark from the first moment of his effective entrance, and the interest grew as the play progressed. It is a moot point whether Mr. Irving is the more successful when he appeals to the heads or to the hearts of his audience. Upon either theory his complete success as Hamlet can be understood. Unconventional, original, as in many respects it was, Mr. Irving's Hamlet bore in every tone, gesture, and glance the amplest evidence of earnest study. The assumed madness, the mingled pity and horror of his mother, the marvellous by-play in the great play-scene, the deliberate, novel, and natural method of the soliloquies, the abandonment of certain stage traditions and the courageous setting of new precedents, all went to prove that the complex nature and conflicting surroundings of the ill-starred Prince had been the subject of close and zestful study upon the part of the actor. The impersonation was an intellectual treat throughout, and at one or two great moments it stirred the emotions also into activity, and it was felt that in Mr. Irving we had as complete and satisfactory a representative of the Danish Prince as even the most *exigéant* critic, the most bigoted and confirmed *laudator temporis acti*, could desire; and the play ran for two hundred representations—the longest run of *Hamlet* on record.

It was during the run of *Hamlet* that a very amusing *contretemps* was avoided by a hair's breadth of good luck. His Excellency the Chinese Ambassador and his attendant, petticoated, pig-tailed, and with the little round button at the top, like the Great Panjandrum, had been "behind the scenes." Upon making their way out from the dim regions they mistook the route, and it was only by the merest accident that they did not suddenly appear on the stage at the most critical moment of the play-scene, when their apparition would probably have "frighted" the King even more than the "false fires" of the players hired by Hamlet; while the effect upon the audience would have been one of those things that can be "better imagined than described."

On June 29th, 1875, *Hamlet* came to an end, to be superseded by *Macbeth* on September 18th, a revival to the full as interesting, as conscientious, as artistically complete, as its predecessor; but which did not, so far as the assumption of the title *rôle* by Mr. Irving, give general satisfaction. The actor was intense as ever, his conception of the ambitious, vacillating Thane was both unconventional and consistent, and there were great moments in the impersonation. But the infirmity of purpose which other actors, with the exception of Edmund Kean, have slurred over, was perhaps insisted upon a little too obtrusively, and without doubt Mr. Irving's peculiarities of gait and elocution were more noticeable than usual; and as these are red rags to a certain class of playgoers, the "occasion to blaspheme" was not wasted upon the enemy. Yet the actor's infinite resources in the way of inventing "business" stood him in good stead, and it was generally admitted that his by-play and facial expressiveness were as mutely eloquent as ever, and that while the conception of the new Macbeth might not be altogether satisfying, the presentment of human passions was lucid and subtle as in other of the actor's creations.

The metamorphosis of Macbeth from a not ignobly ambitious or naturally craven man, by the fascination and spell of superstitious belief in a prophecy which jumped with his own ambition, was finely indicated; so, too, were the remorse, the pitiful terror, the struggle between the higher and lower nature of the man, all the outcome of supernatural influence, acting upon a weak rather than a wicked nature, in a superstitious age—the impersonation proving an interesting, if not an absolutely great, performance.

Then came *Othello*, in February 1876, and again opposing critical forces met and clashed with noisy vigour. Again Mr. Irving had forsaken tradition in costume and in conception of the part; and although there were many touches of the master-hand patent from time to time, the impersonation cannot rank amongst the great successes of the courageous actor. There was undoubtedly an occasional tendency in Mr. Irving's Moor to hysteria, and sometimes a lapse into lachrymosity, which equally robbed Othello of the dignity which is an integral part of his character, read simply by the light of the Shakespearean text. Inevitably the Anti-Irvingites seized with avidity upon the chance to "batten on this Moor," and would, no doubt, have gladly consumed him utterly. But, despite frantic gesticulation and incoherent unintelligibility, despite the whirlwind of passion and the occasionally lugubrious sentimentality and excessive uxoriousness, the indications of dawning jealousy, the sensitive delicacy and self-condemnation with which Othello commissions Iago to set Emilia to spy upon Desdemona, and the sudden tragedy and irresistible pathos of his self-slaughter and death, dragging his dying body to the side of his victim's couch and there falling dead, compelled an admiration which might be withheld from the impersonation as a whole, as in Othello again those irrepressible "mannerisms" thrust themselves unduly to the front, to the delight of captious critics.

After *Othello* had run for some two months, Shakespeare was abandoned for a while, and the Poet Laureate's historical drama, *Queen Mary*, produced in elaborate and imposing fashion, Mr. Irving creating the part of Philip of Spain. In the adaptation and representation of this drama and its hero for the stage there seemed to be a courtesy competition, a rivalry in relinquishment, between the author and the actor. The Laureate sacrificed personage after personage, scene after scene; and, not to be outdone in graceful renunciation, Mr. Irving stripped himself well-nigh bare of his mannerisms, exhibiting a self-control, a moderation, an absence of his usual restless energy, which not only befitted the cool callousness of the royal and heartless King, but revealed the actor in a new, subdued, and quietly-effective light. The cynical cruelty of his treatment of Mary—devoid of all humanity, mocking and merciless, was admirably conveyed, and, as an instance of polished brutality, Philip was a brilliant creation.

After a short and not too successful career, *Queen Mary* gave place to *The Bells* and *The Belle's Stratagem*, a return to melodrama, old comedy, and a Doricourt dressing-gown *de luxe*, which is said to have cost three and a half guineas a yard; to be followed, however, quickly, by a remarkably successful Shakespearean provincial tour, which was the prelude to another Shakespearean revival at the Lyceum, in the shape of the inauguration of the season of 1877 by a production of *Richard III*.

Mr. Irving wisely discarded the mutilated, not to say irreverently tinkered, version of Colley Cibber, and reverted to the original text. His impersonation of the crouch-backed Duke of Gloucester proved to be instinct with intelligence—full of force and fire, the characteristics of the "unpopular King" being clearly marked, while anything like a vulgar exaggeration of his physical deformity was avoided. The cynical cruelty of Richard's forecast of the death of the young princes, the passion of his love-scene with the Lady Anne, were artistic and finished to the last degree. In this new impersonation Mr. Irving fully atoned for any alleged shortcomings in Macbeth and Othello. Richard was well-nigh perfect. All the cynicism and subtlety of the man, as we feel that he must have been, were brought out boldly by the art of the actor, and the curiously interesting, if rather painful, study of a deformed, misshapen, malignant creature, glorying, in a sense, in his own moral and physical warping, was presented with quite exceptional skill. The new Gloucester was a triumph of originality and independence, and was if anything too well furnished with the physiognomical expressiveness and ingenious by-play of which Mr. Irving is so complete a master; but the extreme discretion of the actor in limiting the physical peculiarities of the character, and emphasising the ingenuity of Richard's dissimulation, and Mr. Irving's power of engrossing the imagination of an audience by cleverly conceived "business," were very conspicuous, notably when he studied the map of the battle-field in his tent, before the engagement, in absolute silence, yet without for a single moment losing grip of the complete attention of his audience.

As though in illustration of Diderot's "non-sensibility" theory, the next appearance of Mr. Irving was in the two *rôles* of Joseph Lesurques and Dubosc, in Charles Reade's adaptation of *Le Courier de Lyons*, produced at the Lyceum on May 19th, 1877. For one man to impersonate with convincing realism two such widely divergent characters in the same play was itself a proof of genius. The transformation, in appearance, manner, voice, was most remarkable in the last act, when—after the brutal ruffian Dubosc, uncouth, passionate, hoarse, excited by drink, makes a savage attack upon Fouinard, and then lapses into delirious terror and violent anger with those who have betrayed him, and rushes, distorted and disfigured with rage and fear, behind the opening door—Lesurques enters a few seconds later, calm and self-possessed, the very type of unassuming, well-bred ease. All the passion and brutality of Dubosc were obliterated as though they had never been, and Mr. Irving's ability to convey the agony of a noble-minded man accused of a revolting crime, and hedged in by circumstantial evidence of a convincing kind, and the physical traits common to the two men, differing so utterly in nature, more than justified his following the lead of Charles Kean and taking part in an uncomfortably violent melodrama.

It was on March 9th, 1878, that Mr. Irving appeared for the first time as Louis XI. in Dion Boucicault's adaptation of Casimir Delavigne's drama, and simply took his audience by storm by the brilliant intellectuality of his impersonation. The dramatist has played no courtier's part in dealing with this mean and shifty monarch. Yet there are rags and tatters of regality still clinging to the decrepit, toothless, crafty old King, and now and then they flutter feebly in defence of the right of Louis to a royal title. For the most part the character is despicable, treacherous, malignant, yet Mr. Irving never quite allows his audience to forget that Louis, with all his squalid crouching over the fire, his grim, toothless chuckling over mean triumphs, his malign ill-will, his saturnine humour, his senile incipient decay of body and mind, his doting superstition, his hobbling gait and fantastic mopping and mowing, is still a man, is still a King.

Conditioned by the physical limits of extreme old age, Mr. Irving runs the gamut of human emotions in this part, while the make-up of Louis is perfect—a very nightmare of repellent, malignant senility.

The grim comedy, too, of the scene with the peasants in the third act, and the ghastly terror of the fourth, when the King, in a frenzy of passionate hate, fights the air in the belief that he is slaying the Duc de Nemours, lead up to the really marvellous death-scene in the fifth act—a masterpiece of painful realism, illustrating the utter collapse of physical strength and the pitiless approach of death with a fidelity that is positively appalling. In the opinion of many, Mr. Irving's Louis XI. remains the impersonation of all others most incontestably instinct with genius from first to last,—a quite remarkable effort, intellectually convincing and terrible in its unsparing truth.

This wonderful impersonation was followed by that of Vanderdecken on June 8th, in Messrs. W. G. Wills and Percy Fitzgerald's drama of that name ; but although the character was, in its way, weirdly impressive and admirably picturesque, it did not rank with Mr. Irving's most successful parts, and in the following month the drama was succeeded by *Pickwick*, in which, as Jingle, Mr. Irving again showed a positively ebullient humour.

December 30th, 1878, was a red-letter day in Mr. Irving's career, for on that date the

Lyceum was re-opened under his management —a fact which, while it imposed new obligations, new labours, new responsibilities, upon him, possessed the compensating advantage of giving him an absolutely free hand. Now, if at all, he might be expected to carry out his ideas to their perfect fruition, to prove that his apostrophe of the actor's calling was no mere vapouring affectation.

"How noble the privilege," said Mr. Irving, speaking of the relations of actor and audience, "to work upon these finer—these finest—feelings of universal humanity! How engrossing the fascination of those thousands of steady eyes, and sound sympathies, and beating hearts which an actor confronts, with the confidence of friendship and co-operation, as he steps upon the stage to work out in action his long-pent comprehension of a noble masterpiece!" And now the time had come for the justification of this theory, the fulfilment of this excellent ideal. Fortified by the consciousness of a devoted following and many notable successes in the past, Mr. Irving entered upon his new *rôle* of actor-manager with many points in his favour. His was now the opportunity of making the Lyceum a power—the shrine of culture, the triumph of art, the Mecca of the æsthetic, the intellectual, the intense. Their confidence he already possessed, and he promptly justified it further by the engagement of Miss Ellen Terry—his dramatic "affinity" if there be such a thing in art, and by the revival in splendid fashion of *Hamlet*. He had already proved that the Prince of Denmark, to use his own words, was "flesh and blood, and not a bundle of philosophies," and as such had an unfailing hold upon human sympathies, and upon this memorable first night—anxious as he must have been, burdened with the responsibility of a divided duty in his dual capacity of manager and actor, Mr. Irving re-created the sad and thoughtful Hamlet with a brilliancy and individuality more remarkable than ever. Spurred by a demonstration of loyal attachment such as might have made even a less emotional man than Henry Irving glad and grateful, he excelled himself, and that initial performance of *Hamlet* under the new *régime* was of splendid augury proved the right of the actor to assume absolute control, and sent the audience away with bright anticipations, destined in due course to be realised to the full.

The season of 1879 was more remarkable for revivals than new productions, the only novelty in Mr. Irving's impersonations being Claude Melnotte in *The Lady of Lyons*, produced with mediocre success on April 26th. Mr. Irving is never seen at his best in the *rôle* of a ranting lover, and his Claude, though not without merit and a certain originality of treatment, need not be dwelt upon in the presence of so many assumptions of far more importance.

Somewhat to the dismay of his disciples, Mr. Irving, in his speech at the end of the season, threatened his audience with a revival of some old and effete dramas, such as *The Stranger*, *The Iron Chest*, and *The Gamester*; but happily this infliction was reduced to one only, *The Iron Chest*, produced without conspicuous success on September 27th,—Mr. Irving as Sir Edward Mortimer adding one more figure to his gallery of conscience-stricken criminals.

Following this came a production of *The Merchant of Venice* which proved that Shakespearean drama is never an anachronism, but a thing for all time. The new Shylock was a

MR. IRVING AS SHYLOCK.

brilliant impersonation, conceived in a nobler spirit than convention would have prompted, and carried out with characteristic consistency. Never before had Shylock been invested with so much dignity. Never before had he so clearly embodied all the pathos of a conquered, down-trodden, despised, yet innately great people. Never before had racial characteristics been so strongly marked, yet kept so studiously within the boundary which divides character-acting from caricature. Never before had there been a Shylock for whom it was so easy to feel respect and sympathy. The conventional and vulgar notion of a contemptible Jew usurer, with no soul above his moneybags, no care—beyond the natural instinct of paternal affection—for aught but his ducats, was cast to the winds, and in its place we had a picturesque and pathetic figure, cherishing gold, it is true, but as a shield from Gentile contumely, a sole weapon of defence against powerful and pitiless persecutors ; and even the cruel clamouring for the " pound of flesh lost something of its savagery, conditioned by the actor's new conception of the character.

That Mr. Irving had given minute study to the part and to the play was evident by some bits of "business" not to be found in Shakespeare or in tradition, but which none the less aided the actor's new reading of the part.

The noisy execration of the crowd outside the court, after Shylock's dignified exit, growing fainter by degrees, and the unexpected lifting of the curtain, showing the baffled Jew striding moodily to the home from which, all unknown to him, his daughter had fled, were innovations of genuine artistic value, emphasising the pathos of the new rendition, and compelling sympathy for the defeated, deserted, despairing man.

Whether a Pope of to-day would be disposed to say of Mr. Irving's impersonation as the keen little poet-critic said of Macklin's Shylock— "This is the Jew that Shakespeare drew"— is open to discussion; but it might reasonably be said of Mr. Irving, as of his great predecessor in the part, that he has given us emphatically "his own Jew."

The revival of *The Merchant of Venice*, sumptuous, colourful, satisfying alike to eye and brain, ran for no less than two hundred and fifty nights, and during the latter part of the period Mr. Irving appeared on the same nights as the lover, Count Tristan, in Mr. Wills's *Iolanthe*, a version of *King René's Daughter*, by Herz.

Always possessed, like most people of imaginative minds, by a *penchant* for the mysterious in nature, it was not surprising that the autumn season of 1880 should find Mr. Irving returning to melodramatic mysticism, and producing, on September 18th, Boucicault's version of *Les Frères Corses*. In *The Corsican Brothers*, as Fabien and Louis dei Franchi, Mr. Irving had a comparatively easy task. The picturesqueness and mysterious affinity of the twin brothers, the occult sympathy which is the keynote of the play, were well within the range of his art, and the romantic story, splendidly illustrated by a series of perfectly appointed stage pictures, and invested with peculiar interest by Mr. Irving's assumption of the sympathetic twins, proved popular, and titillated successfully that taste for the creepy and supernatural which is innate in the great majority. The thrilling tremolo of the time-honoured Ghost Melody, the masterly duel in the wood with Château Renaud, and the all-pervading air of supernaturalism, fascinated the town, and enabled Mr. Irving to congratulate himself upon yet one more success.

The new year was destined to see one of

the few new plays produced by Mr. Irving put upon the stage, and on January 3rd, 1881, the Laureate and the Lyceum actor-manager were again in conjunction. But again the two luminaries did not prove as brilliantly attractive as might have been expected. Yet Mr. Irving did all for the play that art and enterprise could suggest. The staging was superb, one scene, the interior of the Temple of Artemis, being almost oppressively solid and magnificent. All that music, incense, elaborate ritual, the mysterious flickerings of sacred fires, the ornate and imposing ceremonial of Pagan religious rites could do, was pressed into the service of the tragedy, but for all that *The Cup* was not an unqualified success. The diction of the work, like everything from the pen of Tennyson, was graceful, polished, faultily faultless; but the theme was unpleasant, unwholesome, and not new. The crime of Camma, in avenging the death of her husband by that of Synorix, has been dealt with on the stage more than once; and, moreover, the *motif* of the play does not lend itself consistently to the Laureate's daintiness of diction, the result being that the speeches sometimes fail to convince—a fatal fault in work presented upon the stage.

As the libertine Synorix, enamoured to madness of the beautiful Priestess of Artemis, Mr. Irving was vigorous, realistic, consistent, and audacious. He left no doubt as to the nature of the sensual Pagan, nor as to the object and passion of his life. The barbarian is a picturesque semi-savage and a bold and effective study, but there is a lack of human sympathy, an absence of verisimilitude about the tragedy, for which no managerial lavishness or perfect actor-craft could atone, and *The Cup* proved likely to remain a play for the study rather than the stage.

On May 2nd, 1881, London playgoers experienced a somewhat exceptional pleasure in a revival of *Othello* at the Lyceum, with Mr. Irving and Mr. Booth playing Iago and the Moor on alternate nights, with Miss Ellen Terry as Desdemona.

Naturally, the Iago of so subtle a master of method and *finesse* as Mr. Irving was anticipated with lively interest, and the event justified the utmost expectations of his admirers. Malign, merciless, yet veiling both qualities under an irresistible air of swaggering candour, the new Iago was daring, original, effective—fertile in fresh "business," restlessly energetic, spirited and vigorous from first to last, and the novel revival proved a success in every sense of the word.

The summer season of 1881 was brought to a close with a representation of *The Hunchback*, with Mr. Irving as Modus, in which *rôle* he displayed a spirit of true comedy, and showed that if he could not play the sentimental lover to advantage he was able to invest the part of a more fanciful wooer with a charm of its own.

On Boxing-night, Mr. Irving revived *The Two Roses*, but although the humour of his impersonation of Digby Grant was riper than ever, the always thin plot and dialogue now proved too weak for popular taste, accustomed to dramatic strong meat; and on March 11th, 1882, an elaborate revival of *Romeo and Juliet* took the stage at the Lyceum, and occupied it, despite much critical dissension, for a hundred and sixty representations.

The beautiful stage-pictures, the perfect stage-management, compelled admiration and commanded success. But the Romeo of Mr. Irving was not ideally excellent. Refined, thoughtful, picturesque, it was an admirable presentment of the graver, sterner side of the character, but the boyish exuberance of passion, the youthful inflammability of temperament, which are the notes of Romeo's nature in the earlier scenes, were sought almost in vain. In his despair, when the boyish, impulsive lover had been sharply urged by sorrow into manhood, Mr. Irving was excellent, and again his by-play and significance of look and gesture and movement were full of intelligence. But the revival is remembered rather as a managerial than a histrionic success.

But Mr. Irving had a lover of another kind in store, and with admirable discretion his next Shakespearean revival was of that happy comedy *Much Ado about Nothing*.

London playgoers were on the tiptoe of expectation as rumours of colossal preparations floated about town, and, while even unbelievers recognised the wisdom of Mr. Irving's latest choice, his votaries anticipated, and rightly, that his Benedick would rank amongst his most consummately artistic impersonations.

And in truth the modern stage has seen

MR. IRVING AS BENEDICK.

nothing finer in pure high comedy than the Benedick of Mr. Irving. The production of *Much Ado about Nothing*, on October 11th, 1882, had been much canvassed, yet even Mr. Irving's most loyal admirers scarcely hoped for such an unqualified triumph. But it was not surprising that the distinction, the perfect refinement and delicate humour, the high-bred courtesy and quick play of fancy of this delightful Shakespearean creation, should find satisfying realisation in the person of so refined and distinguished an actor. And curiously enough, that even the conquest of the cavillers might lack nothing, the actor's "mannerisms" almost absolutely disappeared. The carriage of this new Benedick was grace and courtliness incarnate; the witty verbal thrust and parry were delivered as clearly and intelligibly as the dullard on the one hand and the purist on the other could desire; the whimsical humour and play of fancy which make Benedick a figure for all time were never more fully brought out by an actor or more completely enjoyed by an audience; the creation of Shakespeare, refined, petulant, loyal, affectionate, embittered, but never malignant or mean, was embodied to perfection by Mr. Irving, whose Benedick must always remain one of the most picturesque and absolutely charming of his many impersonations.

In the inevitable speech on the first night of *Much Ado about Nothing* Mr. Irving said: "I am told sometimes that I do wrong to inflict on you the tediousness of Shakespeare—an author whose works some of the wise judges of dramatic art assure us are rather dull and tiresome to a nineteenth-century audience;" but his own inimitable acting made the three-centuries-old play as stirring and as pleasing as it ever could have been in its earliest days.

As a writer of *vers de société* said at the time:—

> "And yet—and yet there are a few
>   Poor fools who fondly cherish
> A hope that what is good and true
>   Will somehow never perish;
> Who hold a stupid threadbare creed,
>   That in our poet's pages
> There lies enough true life indeed
>   To last through all the ages;—
>
> "Who feel his magic to be such,
>   That till the great Hereafter,
> All hearts shall own his gentle touch
>   With weeping and with laughter;—
> Who know that while this world shall last,
>   As long as words are spoken,
> His fame shall never be o'ercast,
>   His kingly sway be broken."

And the success of the revival proved that, as Mr. Irving once said, "Shakespeare is as modern as any playwright of our time. The delightful humour of *Much Ado about Nothing* is as highly relished as the best comedy of our own life and manners."

To this most admirable production succeeded a number of revivals of pieces to be taken to America; and when the time of departure drew near, the whole artistic world of London exerted itself to speed the great actor on his voyage with every token of honour and goodwill. Latterly the farewell banqueting business has been carried by enthusiasts to ridiculous excess, but the great dinner given to Mr. Irving at St. James's Hall, on July 4th, 1883, was unique in stage history. Lord Chief Justice Coleridge presided, and a great crowd, brilliant in literature, the arts, and society, flocked to do honour to the great actor. Five hundred guests, almost without exception men of some distinction, sat down, and some two thousand five hundred applicants for tickets had to be refused. The demonstration was indeed remarkable, and the eloquent speech of the Lord Chief Justice a brilliant tribute to Mr. Irving and his art.

In one clever passage Lord Coleridge summed up the secret of Mr. Irving's power. " It does not become me now," said the Lord Chief Justice, " to analyse critically Mr. Irving's genius, to weigh it in the balance of opinion, or to say that in this or in that it is deficient. To me it is sufficient to be sure that he has an extraordinary and unusual power of conveying the conception of the part which he acts, that he has the power of expressing to me and to others, and making us comprehend, what is in his own mind, and what is his own distinct intellectual conviction."

And in his modest and dignified reply, Mr. Irving seemed happily to hit upon his own secret of success when he said, speaking of actors who would elevate their art : " To effect this creditable purpose they must bring resolute energy and unfaltering labour to their work ; they must be content to spurn delights and live laborious days ; they must remember that whatever is excellent in art must spring from labour and endurance."

This tribute of the representatives of literature, learning, and the arts was followed by a great popular farewell demonstration within the walls of the Lyceum.

With equal courage and discretion Mr. Irving elected to appear that night in two totally dissimilar characters—to give a specimen of his excellent comedy as Doricourt, and of his tragic power as Aram. He was admirable in both, but the real event of the night was the farewell speech, when the audience cheered like people possessed, women did not disguise their emotion, and Mr. Irving himself was profoundly moved. In the face of such a scene the most cynical unbeliever in the stage, save as one of many methods *pour passer le temps*, could not but admit the influence for good or evil it might be in the hands of a "magnetic personality" capable of eliciting such emotion as Mr. Irving.

A short tour in the provinces followed the Lyceum farewell, and at a banquet in Edinburgh Mr. Irving made a clever speech, in which he said : " I am proud of being an actor, and I am proud of my art. It is an art which never dies—whose end and aim is to hold the mirror up to nature, to give flesh and blood to the poet's conception, and to lay bare to an audience the heart and soul of the character which the actor may attempt to portray. It has been the habit of people to talk of Shakespearean interpretations as classics. We hear of classic this and classic that; and if classic is to be refined, and pure, and thoughtful, and natural, then let us be classic by all means; but if in the interpretation of Shakespeare to be classic is to be anything but natural, then the classic is to my thinking a most dangerous rock to strike upon; and as I would be natural in the representation of character, so I would be truthful in the mounting of plays. My object in this is to do all in my power to heighten, and not distract, the imagination—to produce a play in harmony with the poet's ideas, and to give all the picturesque effect that the poet's text will justify."

On October 11th the *Britannic* steamed away from Liverpool to New York, bearing thither Mr. Irving and Miss Terry, after a final "God-speed," in which the very hearts of the people spoke, and which Mr. Irving received with bared and bowed head, touched beyond words.

The American tour, which commenced in New York on Monday, October 29th, 1883, and terminated in the same city on March 30th, 1884, was one round of triumphs, banquets, bouquets, wreaths, speeches, compliments, canvas-back ducks, good-will, good houses, and good cheer. The American interviewers were enraptured with so fertile a subject, the American critics almost unanimous in their praise; the American public generous and appreciative to a fault. A leading critic summed up the secret of the great actor's charm in a phrase, by asserting that he "speaks to the soul and the imagination," and the Americans promptly showed their desire to be credited with the possession of both these good things by crowding the theatres, and so, to the solid satisfaction of all concerned, proving that soulful and imaginative acting is a paying concern.

While Mr. Irving was playing in a town in the "Wild West," he experienced for the first and last time something like discourtesy from the manager of the hotel at which he was stopping.

Mr. Irving had with him his pet dog, "Fussie," between whom and himself a strong affection exists. But the hotel manager was indisposed to accept a dog as a visitor in his establishment, and informed Mr. Irving with unnecessary *brusquerie* that "Fussie" must go.

Protest and expostulation proving wholly vain, Mr. Irving finally precipitated matters by saying calmly: "Very well, bring me my bill. If the dog goes, I go too." The manager then assured Mr. Irving that the dog should be well taken care of outside the hotel if he himself remained, but this did not meet with the actor's approval. He had no desire to leave, but at the same time he was determined not to part with his dog; and all at once an inspiration came to him, and in his coolest fashion he looked at the manager quietly and remarked: "No—that won't do. We'll go. *I* don't mind, but when the dog has gone *what will you do about the rats?*" Apologies, entreaties, humility of manager, slow yielding of Mr. Irving, who remained in the hotel, and heard nothing more of the necessity of "boarding out" his faithful "Fussie."

Mr. Irving made his re-appearance at the Lyceum after his first visit to America on the night of May 31st, 1884, as Benedick, in a revival of *Much Ado about Nothing.* The moment he appeared on the stage, the auditorium became the scene of the wildest enthusiasm. So vigorous and vociferous was the audience in its manifestations of cordial welcome and hearty goodwill, that for a time the progress of the play was interrupted. Mr. Irving rose to the occasion, and acted superbly in what is certainly one of the finest examples of high comedy which has been seen by the present generation of playgoers. And when upon the final fall of the curtain the usual clamorous demand for a speech was made, he delivered a quite admirable little oration, charmingly spoken, conspicuous for its good taste, and commendably free from cheap claptrap about the elevation of the drama and the art of acting, with which, he may have thought, theatrical audiences had been somewhat surfeited. The occasion was a notable one in every way, and offered one more proof of Mr. Irving's popularity, and the irrefragable hold which he had taken upon the sympathies of the public.

On July 8th of the same year a small and ungracious minority saw fit to express a somewhat adverse opinion of the representation of *Twelfth Night*, as revived at the Lyceum by Mr. Irving. Such a discord in the usually harmonious tone of a Lyceum audience jarred unpleasantly upon the ear of *habitués* of the theatre, and inspired Mr. Irving with some unusual comments upon the " strange element" that appeared to be present in the house. The expressions of dissatisfaction were certainly a breach of good taste, and a distinct injustice.

Never in living memory had a play been more magnificently staged; the scenery was exquisite, the dresses superb, the acting, as a rule, excellent. The play dragged, and was, in a degree, a disappointment, but the ironical calls for the " author " were not without significance in this respect, for *Twelfth Night* is not a good acting play. There is so little that is really dramatic in its situations, so little that enlists the sympathy of an audience in the character or circumstances of the principal figures, and the humour is of such a decidedly old-world flavour, that the chances are that if the play were written by a modern dramatist it would go a-begging amongst the managers, and perhaps Mr. Irving showed more courage than discretion in putting upon the stage what he himself has called "one of Shakespeare's most difficult plays." He toned down

MR. IRVING AS MALVOLIO.

the coarseness and clipped the verbiage of the original text with judgment, but for all that the play did not win public favour.

Mr. Irving's Malvolio was quaint, fantastic, grimly humorous. Made up like a cross between

Shylock and Don Quixote—with thin grey hair, a Van Dyck tuft, and an emaciated, oddly-lined, and wrinkled visage, Malvolio, in his prim dress of black and old gold, was a fascinating figure; and in the garden scene, where he is fooled to the top of his bent by Maria's letter purporting to declare her mistress's passion for the steward, Mr. Irving gave us one of the most whimsical bits of humour of the modern stage. The reading of the letter was an excellent piece of comedy, and in the famous cross-gartered scene with Olivia, Malvolio's smile was *impayable*. The scene in the dark room erred on the side of excessive prostration; but in the final outburst, in which the "badly-used Malvolio" rushes from the stage with a threat of revenge, Mr. Irving invested the part with the dignity and passion of a man who feels that he has been grossly and unjustly outraged.

This, in many respects, notable and worthy production, was not, however, destined to hold the stage for long, and on August 23rd Mr. Irving frankly accepted the situation, and commenced with *The Bells* a series of brief revivals of some of his more famous and popular productions, including *Louis XI.* and *Richelieu* and by this means succeeded in finishing the season with *éclat.* The limited success, save in an artistic sense, of *Twelfth Night* must have been somewhat disheartening to Mr. Irving, after the immense pains and expense to which he had gone in its production, but the truth is that Malvolio is a quaint and whimsical creation not to be quite so easily "understanded of the people" as other Shakespearean *rôles* essayed by Mr. Irving with unqualified success. None the less it was appetising to the few, if "*caviare* to the general."

The Lyceum season of 1884 closed on August 28th, and never, perhaps, did Mr. Irving do himself or his subject more ample justice than on the night of his farewell. His Richelieu was a superb impersonation. No shade of the strangely complex nature was lost or slurred. We read as in an open book the character of the wily, yet brave; ambitious, yet tender; pitiless, yet just, disposition of the great Cardinal. Never, too, had the contrast between physical infirmity and mental vigour been more strongly or more subtly defined. There is something infinitely pathetic in the grand wreck which Richelieu becomes in Mr. Irving's hands. We see the story of the loveless life as well as that of the soaring ambition in every gesture of the majestic old man, and the character-study is all the more interesting by reason of the marvellous transitions from the verge of despairing melancholy to the most quaintly cynical humour, or triumphant victory, almost hysterical in its ungovernable ecstasy, over his would-be assassins.

The farewell itself was again a scene to remember—a repetition of all the enthusiasm and affection which were so manifest upon the occasion of the last Lyceum performance prior to his first visit to America.

Mr. Irving's second American tour commenced in Quebec on September 30th, 1884, and terminated in New York on April 4th, 1885, the American public again giving the Lyceum company and their brilliant actor-manager the most cordial welcome.

In connection with this second visit to the States some remarkably free-spoken as well as flattering criticism was indulged in by the

American Press, and in December 1884 the *Philadelphia Record* published something of a curiosity in the way of dramatic criticism. Speaking of the general impression made by Mr. Irving in America, and the attitude adopted towards him, it remarked: "Enlisted as enthusiastic champions on his side is a goodly array of ox-eyed literary daisies, whose nauseating pollen is flung far and wide, stifling the public judgment even as Dalmatian powder chokes a cockroach. Very few of these encephalitic growths, however, project their looming mass upon the horizon of Philadelphia, and Mr. Irving has been generally judged and approved in this city with due regard to his merits and demerits as well." This was frank, and, in its own way, flattering; moreover it had the merit of possessing a distinct flavour of truth.

During the same tour, in the following April, an amusing incident occurred at the Star Theatre, New York, during a representation of *Twelfth Night*. It was when Malvolio, fooled to the uttermost, is being roasted by Sir Toby, Fabian, and Maria, and has to ask them, " Do you know what you say?" As fate would have it, Mr.

Irving put a distinct accent on the "you," and as the phrase was drily enunciated—"Do *you* know"—the audience gave noisy vent to their delight in a burst of laughter. Mr. Irving paused a moment, evidently a little embarrassed at making this unexpected point. Then he repeated it, to the provocation of another roar, and it was only in the wings that he learned that he had unwittingly parodied *The Private Secretary*.

Upon the departure of Mr. Irving from America an example of the enthusiasm which he evoked may be gathered from a short excerpt from a poetical address penned by the well-known critic, Mr. William Winter:—

"Now fades across the glimmering deep, now darkly drifts away
  The royal monarch of our hearts, the glory of our day:
  The pale stars shine, the night winds sigh, the sad sea makes
    its moan,
  And we, bereft, are standing here, in silence and alone.
  Gone every shape of power and dread his magic touch could
    paint;
  Gone haunted Aram's spectral face and England's martyred
    saint,
  Gone Mathias of the frenzied soul, and Louis' sceptred guile,
  The gentle head of poor Lesurques, and Hamlet's holy smile."

The delicate flattery of this is as exceptional

a tribute as even a "royal monarch" of the stage could desire or expect.

A notable instance of Mr. Irving's success as a diplomatist occurred upon the occasion of his return from America, in the spring of 1885. The night of Saturday, May 2nd, was trebly interesting. There was the question: Had Mr. Irving lost touch with the public during his prolonged absence? Then it was doubtful how far the innovation of booking seats in the pit and gallery would be approved; and, during Mr. Irving's absence, a new and notable Hamlet had appeared to invite comparison.

The reception awarded to Mr. Irving was cordial, affectionate; his performance refined, touching, full of subtlety and poetic feeling, always excellent, occasionally great; and the audience recognised this heartily. But when the curtain fell for the last time, and Mr. Irving made the usual "speech," the Old Pitites and the New Pitites grew vociferous. An unusual storm raged in the Lyceum, and Mr. Irving, whose bearing throughout was in admirable taste, very properly said that it was not the time to arrive at any definite decision. But the storm still raged, until, by one of his flashes of genius, Mr. Irving turned the situation to his advantage by quoting *Hamlet* with a grace and charm which simply won the whole house, summing up the affair by saying, with inimitable courtesy of tone and bearing: "What so poor a man as Hamlet is may do, to express his love and friending to you, God willing, shall not lack."

It would be difficult to imagine and ungrateful to desire anything more exquisitely beautiful, though almost painfully pathetic, than the representation of Mr. W. G. Wills's play *Olivia*, as revived at the Lyceum on May 30th, 1885. *The Vicar of Wakefield*, Goldsmith's perfect and classic story of woman's love and trust sacrificed to man's passion and perfidy, has formed the *motif* of innumerable plays, poems, and pictures, so tempting is it to the artistic temperament. Mr. Wills kept closely to Goldsmith's story, but the simple, nervous, direct, and graceful diction was largely his own. There was no fine writing, no straining after effect— a touching simplicity and tender delicacy pervaded the whole work; the tone was consistent, and the pathetic character of the play relieved by the only humour possible in such a theme —the gentle playfulness of the Vicar, whose humour is as softly lambent and as harmless as summer lightning, and the coy and simple loves of Moses and Polly. The story is so full of tender pathos that it would have been barbarous to have marred its tearful charm with bucolic witticisms or rustic buffoonery, and although the Lyceum version of *The Vicar of Wakefield* must be classed amongst the pleasures of melancholy, the pity and sympathy which it compelled prove the purity and beauty of the work.

Mr. Irving's Dr. Primrose was a delight. The Vicar proved as gentle, lovable an old man as Goldsmith's ideal. Full of simple dignity, invested with a rare charm of old-world grace and courtesy, and showing, when occasion demands, a sturdy manliness and righteous indignation, Dr. Primrose must ever rank amongst Mr. Irving's happiest impersonations. The almost idolatrous affection of the old Vicar for his beautiful and gentle daughter; his happiness in her love; his despair at her flight; his dignified rebuke of her betrayer; his passionate welcome to his erring child; his simple piety and faith —all were painted with marvellous fidelity to nature, all bore the unmistakable stamp of genius. At one or two critical moments Mr. Irving's individuality was perhaps a little too pronounced, but the impersonation as a whole was a fine one and a faithful.

The production of Mr. W. G. Wills's version of *Faust*, on the night of Saturday, December 19th, 1885, was remarkable for two points: it gave London playgoers a spectacle such as even the Lyceum stage had never before presented, and it further gave them a Mephistopheles without equal in the history of the stage. Beyond these two features there was little in the new *Faust* that had not been done, and done as well, before. But what exceptions these two points were!

Weird and almost superhumanly vivid as must have been the imagination which conjured up the unholy revels of Walpurgis Night on the Brocken, its wildest dreams were realised upon the Lyceum stage; and grimly humorous, splendidly Satanic, as was Goethe's conception of Mephistopheles, the terrible and fantastic

MR. IRVING AS MEPHISTOPHELES.

creation was embodied with perfect fulness and fidelity by Mr. Irving.

Critics and commentators without number have so thoroughly thrashed out the *motif* and construction of the great poem upon which this latest dramatic version was based, that it is only necessary to deal with what was actually put before the audience by Mr. Wills and Mr. Irving.

Mr. Wills, in his share of the work, showed a commendable regard for the integrity of the original. It was Goethe anglicised; and even when the adapter found it necessary to strike out a path for himself, he did so with discretion, and diverged as little as possible from the sequence and spirit of the poem. Mr. Wills gave, perhaps, a little too much prominence to the pessimistic side of the tragedy. Mephistopheles was so pitilessly sardonic; Margaret's farewell cry, "Heinrich! Heinrich!" so rich in hope and promise, was expunged, and the curtain fell upon a Faust dragged to perdition by Mephistopheles, and without apparent hope of redemption from the purgatorial fires; yet that is perhaps a detail which would bring the great play to a more artistic as well as a happier climax.

The sardonic *diablerie* of Mephistopheles, as shown by Mr. Irving in every gesture, glance, and word, was marvellous. The sense of power conveyed by the cruel face made the undercurrent of mocking humour the more comprehensible. It was evident, from the moment when the grim, cynical features peered through the cloud of vapour in Faust's study, that Mephistopheles was so sure of his prey, that his power over his victim was so absolute, that he could afford to unbend; that the rigid muscles could well relax into a sardonic smile; that the lips, curling in devilish scorn, could condescend to juggle with words, to taunt poor purblind man, to sneer at a weak woman, to bandy repartee with and fool to the top of her bent an amorous Martha. The potency of the Mephistopheles of Mr. Irving was so all-pervading, so palpable, that it was not surprising that he played with his victim, and thrust him down to perdition with a laugh.

Now and then the humour of Faust's tempter smacked just an atom of ordinary comedy; yet when Mephistopheles was on the stage all else sank into insignificance, and this, be it said, not because of undue or inartistic obtrusiveness, but by sheer force of the fascination of the figure.

Although it may appear a doubtful compliment, it is a fact that Mr. Irving's physique proved peculiarly adaptable for the impersonation. The minimum of make-up could and did produce a perfect Mephistopheles. The glittering eyes, the curiously heavy brows, the long, gaunt visage, all the materials for an ideal Mephistopheles were there, and the actor was too true an artist not to take advantage of them to the full.

Even the perennially discussed individualities of style stood Mr. Irving in good stead in the new *rôle*, the Evil Spirit being usually credited with a cloven hoof and a slight lameness, which fully justified Mr. Irving's gait in the part.

It was in Faust's study—a grim chamber, hung about with stuffed monsters, crammed with scientific apparatus, and illumined only by a flickering lamp, that Mephistopheles first appeared, coming from a cloud of mist which hissed and curled up into the dim shadows of the roof. Mephistopheles then looked more like Dante than himself, and in this character he first tempted his victim, and gave the audience a fine little bit of grim comedy when he donned the robe of Faust and gave the student who called in quest of the great scholar some diabolically cynical advice about women. In the scene in St. Lorenz Platz, despite its splendid grouping, Mephistopheles took part in somewhat too pantomimic business with the drunken revellers; but the scene at the City Wall, in which Mephistopheles taunted Faust with his super-sensitiveness, and sneered him into sin, was excellently done. So too were the capital bit of gruesome comedy in Martha's house, when Mephistopheles, with mischievous humour and mocking cynicism, told the trumped-up tale of the death of her husband; and the great garden-scene, with its irritating alternations of dialogue, but also its irresistible Mephistophelean humour.

The episode in the church, when Mephistopheles whispered evil counsels into the ear of the praying Margaret, was subtle and effective.

The stage management of this act throughout was beyond praise, and the effect of the final moment, when Mephistopheles was alone upon the stage, crouching beneath a statue of the Madonna, trying to shut out the sound of the holy music, and at the same time wearing an expression of devilish triumph and malignancy, was superb.

But perhaps the crowning triumph of Mr. Irving, both as actor and manager, was reached in the remarkable scene upon the summit of the Brocken, where Walpurgis Night revels, weird, fantastic, grim, ghastly, yet picturesque beyond description, revealed Mephistopheles at the very apex of his mad wickedness. Revelling in the unholy antics, he stalked and hobbled about the stage, caressing foul goblins and repulsive apes, calling legions of spirits with a word, and dismissing them with an imperious gesture, and at last standing amidst lurid flames and utter desolation, alone, triumphant, devilish.

The " Revisioners" having abolished hell, Mr. Irving did his best in this scene to show what it might have been, and neither Dante nor Doré ever had a more ghastly, lurid, appalling vision, and perhaps no audience ever heard a more perfectly inhuman laugh of triumph in its infernal cynicism, than that given by Mephistopheles when the lovers meet in the garden after he himself had been driven cowering from Margaret's presence by the uplifted cross.

Faust had, as it deserved, a quite stupendous success. Indeed, it seemed as if Mr. Irving's jocular reference in his speech upon the first night of its production, to the introduction of new features from time to time, so that an element of variety might be imported into its six-hundred-nights' run, would in all sober earnest prove prophetic. As a matter of fact the play ran right through the season of 1886, and was revived again in unbroken sequence, continuing the run until April 23rd, 1887, and it was not until the 244th representation, on November 15th, 1886, that Mr. Irving even deemed it politic to introduce the promised new element in the shape of the introduction of the famous scene in the witches' kitchen, which, needless to add, was put upon the stage with characteristic thoroughness.

The withdrawal of *Faust* was followed by a series of short revivals of favourite pieces, among them being *The Merchant of Venice*, *The Bells*, *Pickwick*, and *Olivia;* the last performance of the season, on July 16th, being that of *The Merchant of Venice*, in which Mr. Irving surpassed himself as Shylock.

But prior to this a notable performance, though only a single representation of the drama, was held at the Lyceum for the benefit of the poet and dramatist, Dr. Westland Marston.

The event proved an instance of Mr. Irving's conscientiousness as an artist, and kindness as a man, when on the afternoon of June 1st he revived the sombre drama *Werner* for the benefit of his old friend. With a thoroughness which was peculiarly graceful under the circumstances, Mr. Irving went to as much trouble and expense in the provision of dresses and scenery as if an extended run were expected. Special incidental music was composed, and the drama was strengthened by a new and effective scene written at Mr. Irving's suggestion by Mr. Frank Marshall. The result was not only the realisation of the substantial sum of £800 for the *bénéficiaire*, but also an artistic success.

As Werner Mr. Irving once more engrossed the attention of the audience whenever he was upon the stage. Not only was his appearance curiously impressive, his white hair, dark, restless eyes, and incessant movement compelling them to follow him in every gesture, by which, quite as much as by the spoken text, he reveals the sensitive nature of the man. Excellent in the earlier part of the play, irritated and rendered morbidly petulant under the pressure of poverty; more excellent still in the curious reasoning as to the varying degrees possible in crime, in which Werner enunciates arguments to be adopted with terrible logic later on by his guilty son, Mr. Irving, with true artistic instinct, reserved the superlative force of his acting for the final scene, and so confirmed and consummated the success of one more remarkable and thoughtful impersonation.

Mr. Irving's third American tour, which was also destined to prove successful, commenced in New York on November 7th, 1887, and on his return from the States he reopened the Lyceum

MR. IRVING AS ROBERT MACAIRE. MR. WEEDON GROSSMITH AS
JACQUES STROP.

with a revival of *Faust*, following this with a revival of *The Amber Heart* and *Robert Macaire* on May 23rd, which sufficed to fill the theatre until the close of the season on July 7th, when, in the customary speech, Mr. Irving promised *Macbeth* as his next Shakespearean revival.

This promise he redeemed on December 29th, when the great play was revived with elaborate and magnificent stage effects and scenery, and ran throughout the following season. For the first time since his appearance upon the London stage, Mr. Irving was compelled to absent himself through illness during part of the run of this play, from January 17th to the 26th, 1889, during which period Macbeth was excellently impersonated by Mr. Hermann Vezin.

On April 26th, Mr. Irving and his company had the honour of appearing before the Queen and the Prince and Princess of Wales at Sandringham, in *The Bells* and the trial scene from the *Merchant of Venice*, and Mr. Irving was the recipient of much flattering criticism from his royal audience.

Ever a diplomat of diplomats, Mr. Irving was not the man to let the centenary of the French Revolution pass without a discreet dramatic

MR. IRVING AS MACBETH.

exploitation of its artistic and financial possibilities. With all the world flocking to Paris to the great Exhibition, and crossing the Channel to round off their holiday in London, what so safe a card to play as one directly concerned with the great celebration? With a little literary doctoring at the hands of Mr. W. H. Pollock, there was an old Adelphi drama ready to hand, and if Benjamin Webster, with his comparatively limited spectacular resources, could make Watts Phillips's melodrama *The Dead Heart* a success, why should not Mr. Irving, with his prestige, his popularity, his splendid facilities, all aided by the sentiment of the centennial celebration, do the same? That he did so, and more, is now a matter of history.

Nor was this result surprising. The curtain had not long risen on the night of September 28th, 1889, when it was evident not only that Mr. Irving was determined to give the revival the advantage of all that taste, research, and lavish outlay could command, but that there was, after all, so much humanity in the old play that it might well have held the stage again awhile, even without the attraction of such magnificent mounting and the adventitious aid of the Revolution centenary. Full of stirring incidents and opportunities for a potent and astute stage-manager to evolve marvels of spectacular effect, and dealing with a period absolutely crowded with emotional conditions, *The Dead Heart* could scarcely fail to at least excite some popular interest. Staged and acted as it was at the Lyceum, it became the sensation of the autumn season. Opinions might differ as to the realism of Mr. Irving's dishevelled locks and flowing beard, and the rapidity of his recovery of something like reason after his release from eighteen years' incarceration in the Bastile—but the surging mob of maniacal men and unsexed women which filled the stage with its inarticulate cries, its mad dancing of the Carmagnole, and inhuman gambols at the taking of the Bastile, and the picturesque nobility of Robert Landry as he awaited his voluntary martyrdom on the scaffold, were very real and very fascinating. And so this dramatic picture of the Revolution, with its central group of interesting figures all "palpitating with actuality," was "restored"

MR. IRVING AS ROBERT LANDRY

by the great actor-manager, and all London rushed to see it.

In Robert Landry Mr. Irving was once more able to display the artistic versatility in a single *rôle* which is one of his strong points. In the prologue Robert Landry was the joyous lad —handsome, frank, debonair, irresistible, an artist-patriot almost reckless in his boyish self-abandonment, an ardent lover, with, as he believes, a long vista of happy life stretching away before him. Suddenly all is changed : the young patriot is thrown into the Bastile, not again to see the light of the sun until eighteen years later, when, upon the seizure of the prison by the Revolutionaries, he rushes, dazed and blinded, back to light and life and liberty. But his bewilderment is rather physical than mental, and ere long he recovers his wits, only to gain a knowledge bitterer than death. The woman in whose faith and constancy he trusted has married. Then, with inimitable art, Mr. Irving depicted Robert Landry as a man restored to life and freedom, but valuing neither, as his heart was dead within him.

From this stage to the sublime self-sacrifice

with which the drama closes, Mr. Irving's impersonation became consistently impressive. His first callous indifference to the prayer of his old love for the life of her son, the young Comte de St. Valéry, now in Landry's power and condemned to death—an indifference intensified into pitilessness by the knowledge that his old-time enemy, the Abbé Latour, was the young man's tutor; the terrific duel to the death with the Abbé, after the discovery of his perfidy in the old days, in keeping back Landry's reprieve; his ultimate relenting for the sake of the effort which the young Comte's father had made for him eighteen years before, and the final sublime sacrifice upon the scaffold, were all intense and emotional in the extreme, and the play was made, like almost everything touched by Mr. Irving, an artistic and financial success. The complexities of Landry's character made the part a satisfying study for the critical; the spectacular magnificence delighted the lovers of display; the strong humanity of the story appealed to all, and *The Dead Heart* revival became one more proof that Mr. Irving had not rashly undertaken the task of gauging

MR. IRVING AS RAVENSWOOD.

public taste as a manager, as well as gratifying it as an actor.

Upon the night of Saturday, September 20th, 1890, Mr. Irving produced with magnificent scenic effects and unqualified artistic success Mr. Herman Merivale's blank verse play, *Ravenswood*, based upon Sir Walter Scott's story, "The Bride of Lammermoor," himself creating the part of Edgar, the Master of Ravenswood. Although the drama diverged in many points from the story, the spirit of the original was admirably preserved; and although there was a certain inevitable sombreness and gloom about a play in which the principal characters are so obviously the puppets of a terrible and fatal destiny, the whole work was instinct with a dignity, a pathos, a grace, a romance, which threw the glamour of poesy over even the most harrowing scenes, raising them to pure tragedy and making them an absorbing and fascinating study.

As the Master of Ravenswood Mr. Irving added a noble and beautiful crea ion to his *répertoire*. Whether as the orphaned and beggared son of the earlier scenes, in which there is a Hamlet-like intensity of filial affection and bitter sense of wrong; as the chivalrous, tender, passionate lover whose wooing is idyllic in its grace and charm; as the despairing, heart-broken man who reels in the weakness of fever to the aid of his betrothed wife, only to find that she has agreed to wed another; or as the desperate, wretched soul racked by the sense of loss and the suspicion of treachery, he was perfect in his subtle art, his personal distinction, the inimitable refinement and intellectuality of his conception of the part. A compound of Hamlet and Romeo, with all the miserable sense of impotence to avenge the wrongs of a dead father, and all the ill-starred love for a girl whose family is at deadly feud with his own, Edgar, the Master of Ravenswood, is a powerful and tragic conception, and Mr. Irving brought out all the intense pathos and beauty of the *rôle* with consummate art. Even in his inarticulate cries of scorn and subtle indications of an effort at self-control under the taunts of Lady Ashton, Mr. Irving gave ample proof of the perfection and delicate finish of his art; and it speaks eloquently for his genius that, despite the innately and persistently melancholy nature of Edgar, he never failed to grip the attention and compel the sympathy of the audience from the moment of his first impressive entry upon the occasion of his father's funeral, when with a stern sadness he commands the bearers to "set down their burden" that he may commune with his dead, until that other solemn moment, when he finally rushes from the stage on learning the death of Lucy, with the wild cry that he must "hold her dead corse in his arms—the rest is nothing!"

Mr. Irving's genius both as actor and manager was patent in every detail of the play and of his own impersonation, and *Ravenswood*, in the face of obvious difficulties, proved a dual triumph and so great a delight to cultivated playgoers that it is no longer difficult to understand the zeal of those enthusiasts who gathered around the pit-door of the theatre ten hours and a half before the opening of the doors. Such acting as Mr. Irving's, and such exquisite beauty as that of the mounting of *Ravenswood*, are just those things which cannot be bought too dearly. A keen pleasure at the time, such an experience remains a notable memory for ever, and the playgoing public owe a debt to Mr. Irving for artistic and emotional delights which no amount of cordial recognition of the great work which he has done for the stage can ever pay.

On December 20th and 27th, 1890, Mr. Irving, reverted once more to his powerful impersonation of the haunted burgomaster Mathias in a revival of *The Bells*, which proved to have lost no iota of its hold upon the lovers of weird and grim melodramatic acting of the first school, and upon January 5th, 1891, he revived *Much Ado about Nothing* in the superb fashion of his former revival of this exquisite play, and again delighted his audience with the perfection of high comedy as Benedick.

MR. WILSON BARRETT, FROM A PHOTOGRAPH BY J. THOMSON, 70, GROSVENOR STREET.

"There's a divinity that shapes our ends." *Hamlet*

Wilson Barrett

WILSON BARRETT.

AN enthusiast for the drama and everything connected with it from his earliest youth—as he told his audience upon a notable occasion—he would hurry into the pit of the Princess's Theatre to satisfy his theatrical cravings with the contemplation of Charles Kean in one or other of his great impersonations, it is yet only during the last decade that the name of Wilson Barrett has become a household word with London playgoers. But during that decade he has worked wonders by sheer force of talent, courage, and perseverance.

Until September 20th, 1879, when he appeared as the advocate Pomerol, in *Fernande*, at the opening of the Court Theatre under his management, Mr. Barrett had been, if not exactly wasting his fragrance on the desert air, at least only undergoing a training, valuable enough as it proved, in the provinces, where he speedily acquired a name as an enterprising and discreet manager, and an actor of more than average intelligence and promise.

Mr. Barrett's first appearance was at Halifax in 1864, when he was eighteen years old, and he received a guinea a week as "general utility," with a dance between the acts. But after six weeks he was entrusted with a leading juvenile part, having the book handed to him half an hour before midnight one night, with instructions to copy out, learn, and act his part upon the following evening. Little then did the young actor think of the time to come when, as lessee of a great London theatre, he should within the compass of a very few years pay no less a sum than £75,000 in authors' fees alone.

It was during these provincial wanderings that Mr. Barrett had an amusing experience while playing Triplet in *Masks and Faces*, which afforded somewhat of an argument against absolute realism on the stage.

In the attic scene, in which good-natured Peg Woffington sends a pie for the delectation of the poor broken-down gentleman and his starving little ones, Mr. Barrett, knowing that the children who appeared with him were not too well accustomed to good solid meals, took care to provide a genuine beefsteak pie each night, which they consumed with unmistakable gusto, he, too, taking his share of the realistic meal. But one night, no sooner had Triplet inserted the knife in the crust of the pie than a malodorous savour assailed his nostrils, and compelled him to "make believe" that he was enjoying the welcome food.

Not unnaturally, he thought that the children would not be so squeamish, and duly gave them their portions. But to his horror they remained upon the plates untouched, and the curling lip of disdain was the only indication which they gave of their knowledge of its presence. The situation was critical. "Eat, you little beggars, eat!" said the actor, *sotto voce*. But it was no good. Nature asserted itself over art, and for once Mistress Woffington's bounty was unappreciated.

The incident reminds one of the conceited young London star who, when touring in the provinces, arrogantly demanded a real chicken in one of his scenes, instead of a "property" make-believe. The stage-manager, after bearing with his upstart ways as long as he could, quietly said at last: "All right, Mr. Dash; I'll remedy it to-morrow. You play the part of a man who is murdered, don't you?" "Yes," returned the star. "Very good," replied the manager, "*I'll take care that the poison is real!*"

As some men are born great, so, it would seem, are some born to a certain class of dramatic work. If ever there was a born actor of romantic drama of the robust and picturesque school, Mr. Wilson Barrett is the man. An expressive, handsome face, well-set-up figure, resonant voice, and considerable grace and dignity of bearing, he is the *beau idéal* of a hero of romance. In an age by no means insusceptible to the merits of muscularity, Mr. Barrett's admirable physique gave him an initial advantage. To this were added distinct talent of a very high order, courage, modesty, pluck, good taste, and minor characteristics equally charming, with the result that when he came to London he was seen, and he conquered.

With excellent discretion Mr. Barrett, having gauged his strength and tested his capacity in the art of acting, quickly identified himself with a particular class of character, only diverging from it now and again into some widely dissimilar field, as if of set purpose to show the public that he could, an he would, extend the compass of his artistic efforts.

But when his excursions into the realm of pure tragedy and Shakespearean fantasy are remembered, and all due credit is given to the actor for impersonations of quite exceptional merit, the fact remains that the mention of the name of Wilson Barrett calls up in the minds of the majority of practised playgoers memories of romantic heroes—romantic in their essential attributes, whether ruffling in the lace and velvet of a Lord Harry Bendish; pacing in barbaric pride or weary dignity in the white and classic robes of Claudian; staggering in picturesque dissipation as Wilfred Denver; moving with measured stately steps, clad in the spotless robes of the patriot Junius; passing through dire suffering with manly pluck and pathetic power as Harold Armytage; or posing with facile grace as Jack Hearne, the Romany Rye, or gipsy gentleman—always romantic, always suffering unmerited ills, always sure to emerge triumphant in the final act, as becomes so virile, so virtuous, so sympathetic a hero.

Mr. Barrett's career has not been one of unclouded success, but it is on record to his honour that he never put a play upon the stage, or assumed a new part, without doing his utmost to make both deserve, even if they did not command, success. And it is yet more to his credit that even in those cases where the financial result has not been of the greatest, if he has been convinced of the intrinsic worthiness of the work he was presenting he has at least kept it upon the boards sufficiently long for it to achieve an artistic success.

Courage, enterprise, honest endeavour, and thoughtful study, these have been the dominant notes in Mr. Barrett's stage policy, and, as such excellent qualities should do, they have won for their possessor an enviable position and reputation in the record of the stage of to-day, as well as a large and enthusiastic following.

Certain creations which the persistent playgoers of the last ten years will instinctively recall, would have been, if not impossible, at least very much less satisfying, in the hands of any other player of the period, not for lack of adequate histrionic capacity, but because Mr. Barrett, like all strong personalities, possesses certain conspicuous characteristics, thoroughly individual, though not eccentric enough to have been stigmatised as mannerisms, which have lent distinction to the *rôles* he has assumed, adding alike to their immediate effectiveness and to their enduring quality. To illustrate this more clearly, it is only necessary to mention the brilliant creation of Wilfred Denver, in *The Silver King*, a character which not only afforded Mr. Barrett magnificent opportunities, but which, probably, no living actor could have created with quite such convincing completeness.

As actor and as manager Mr. Barrett has given such repeated evidence of talent, of lavish expenditure of his own powers and discreet enlistment of those of others, of scholarly care and artistic feeling as regards the text and staging of the plays which he has produced; of being, in effect, "thorough" in everything to which he puts his hand, that he has won the respect of all who recognise and value clever and conscientious work for the stage; while his personal charm of manner and obvious strivings to please the public and give them of his best, have won for him a large circle of enthusiastic admirers and loyal friends, as well as an honoured place in the ranks of the foremost actors of his day.

After M. Pomerol, in *Fernande*, ensued a number of brief impersonations at the Court and Princess's Theatres, including a thoughtfully played Claude de Courcy in *Courtship;* a quiet, careful, and effective Henri de Sartorys, in *Frou-Frou;* an original, boldly unconventional, and excellent Mercutio, full of humanity, and revealing traits hitherto for the most part hidden by actors of the part; a dignified, earnest study of John Stratton, in *The Old Love and the New;* and a remarkable representation of a youthful priest, as Friar John, in *Juana*, an impersonation which undoubtedly, and in the face of adverse fortune, helped to force upon the perception of *habitués* of the theatre the fact that a new actor of quite exceptional merit—earnest, intelligent, with alert brain, a mastery of his craft, and every quality necessary to command success—had arisen in the dramatic firmament, and must hereafter take a permanent place in the critical chart.

Rarely has there been so much admirable blank verse wasted, permitted to die and be buried away out of sight and out of the memory of most, as in the case of Mr. Wills's beautiful but sombre drama *Juana*. Yet those who were present on the night of its production at the Court Theatre, on May 7th, 1881, must remember well the power with which Madame Helena Modjeska held the audience enthralled in the pathetic mad scene in the second act.

The play, constructed as unskilfully as it was gracefully written, was a failure, except in an artistic sense, and has only been revived once since, and then without success. But in it Mr. Barrett gave the public an excellent piece of work as Friar John, in which he presented a thoughtful, consistent, and dignified picture of a high-minded young priest, tried by conflicting emotions, and declaimed with admirable art some of the most beautiful passages in a play rich in poetical diction.

But neither the pathos of Madame Modjeska, the elocution and art of Mr. Barrett, nor the picturesqueness of monkish processions and the weirdness of "ordeal by touch," could save the play, which, containing much beautiful work, the loss of which is a loss to dramatic literature, chiefly served to afford the public an opportunity of recognising an actor of rare promise in Mr. Wilson Barrett.

The first great success in the direction of that class of powerful romantic melodrama of contemporary life, which Mr. Wilson Barrett produced for a time with such marked success, was made by *The Lights o' London*, written by Mr. G. R. Sims, and produced at the Princess's Theatre on Saturday, September 10th, 1881. In *The Lights o' London* the broad human sympathy, the acute perception of the noble and the beautiful in common life and common people, the hatred of social shams, the love of all that is true and kindly, which marked the works of Dickens, were all present ; and beneath all the pathos and tragedy, the sin and suffering, the passion and the pain of the drama, ran a pleasant vein of humour, conceived in the true Dickens spirit. It was not left merely for the " gods " to recognise the strong situations and genuine value of the play. The orthodox affectation of languid cynicism in the stalls was lost in one great wave of sympathy, which spread throughout the house as situations of intense power and pathos followed each other with overpowering rapidity. The story of *The Lights o' London* is infinitely sad, but the humorous element skilfully relieves it; and the audience, as it followed the fortunes of the hero, Harold Armytage, felt that they were looking at life as it is, with all its strange vicissitudes and paradoxes, its joys and sorrows, its virtue and its vice, its trials and temptations, its sufferings and its triumphs. The story of the scapegrace but noble-hearted son, discarded by a stiff-necked father, and of the terrible troubles which follow, is excellently told, and in Harold Armytage Mr. Wilson Barrett was fitted with a part which enabled him to do full justice to his powers. His fine face, instinct with intelligence, harmonised with the pure and manly sentiments of which he was the mouthpiece; his resonant, musical voice and good presence lent dignity and strength to countless powerful situations, and his delivery of certain didactic passages, which in less skilful hands might have savoured somewhat of platitude, was marked by a nice appreciation of the limits of effective moralising. There was human nature in the play and the acting, and the result was a pronounced success.

On Saturday, June 10th, 1882, Mr. Barrett created the part of Jack Hearne, in Mr. G. R. Sims's gipsy drama *The Romany Rye*. Needless to say that as the Romany Rye, or gipsy gentleman, Mr. Barrett had a part which was calculated to display his physical attractions and artistic skill to the uttermost. The drama is a sensational *mélange*, in which burglary, murder, love, jealousy, gipsies, dog-fanciers, gin-shops, underground cellars, the pure air of the country, the pestilential effluvia of St. Giles's slums, courage and cowardice, picturesque manhood, primed with all the virtues, and flash villainy, treacherous and cruel, sweet girlhood and degraded womanhood, the beauties of the Thames by moonlight and the filthy dens of the depraved and brutal in Ratcliffe Highway, are in one drama blent, and Zolaistic naturalism is the *mot d'ordre*. Mr. Barrett's part involved perhaps greater muscular than mental strain, for it must be exhausting for even a hero of melodrama to be perpetually rescuing virtue in distress, struggling very literally against overwhelming odds, and facing imminent peril and incalculable hardship ere justice is done and he comes to his own. But Jack Hearne was a manly, dashing fellow from first to last, the performance a really powerful one, and the whole production a signal success.

In its particular school of work Mr. Wilson Barrett never did anything finer than his creation of the striking character of Wilfred Denver, in Messrs. Henry Arthur Jones and Henry Herman's clever drama *The Silver King*, produced at the Princess's Theatre on December 26th, 1882. A handsome scapegrace, a slave, when we first meet him, to drink and dissipation, yet never lacking in a certain innate refinement and nobility; weak rather than vicious, and led by his weakness to a tragic catastrophe, Wilfred Denver is an incarnate homily, but one that is never dull, never even didactic. Admirably written and full of splendid situations, *The Silver King* marked a new era in romantic melodrama, and furnished Mr. Barrett with quite one of his finest parts. The spectacle of a not innately bad man labouring under the awful belief that in a fit of drunken delirium he has committed murder is pathetic enough, but it is brightened in this case by the extreme tenderness and affection of Denver for his wife and children; and a note of intensely true pathos is struck when the man, flying for his life, yearns to kiss his sleeping children, takes a hesitating step or two towards their room, and then, with a broken-hearted cry that he is unworthy to touch them, goes out into his compulsory exile.

Nor is the moment when Denver first discovers the dead body of Geoffrey Ware, and believes that he has killed him, less effective. In it, Mr. Barrett rises to pure tragedy, and his horror is a thing not to be easily forgotten. When, after attaining fortune in

America, Wilfred Denver, the Silver King, returns to find his wife and children in dire poverty, and can only help them secretly, Mr. Barrett's pathos is of just the right tone—never whining or lachrymose, but as manly as it is true. Indeed, in all the light and shade of a picturesque but very exacting part, the actor proves himself to be a master of his art and a faithful student of humanity.

The character of Denver is conditioned by circumstances of peculiar gravity and terror, yet the sympathy of the audience is never alienated. A scapegrace brought to reason by the imagined commission of murder; dead to the world and all dear to him; returning with all the material elements of happiness, yet unable even to declare to his wife and children the fact that he is alive—rarely, indeed, has a story been told which appeals at once so strongly to the imagination and the humanity of an audience. And in the lowest depths of Denver's degradation there is an inextinguishable refinement; the pathos is true, and the mental agony so vividly depicted by Mr. Barrett as to ensure that the creation will remain one of the most touching studies of the contemporary stage.

The make-up of Mr. Barrett in the third act was a masterpiece of artistic skill, which led Mr. Henry Arthur Jones to remark to him at rehearsal, "No one could possibly *be* half as good as you *look!*"

A curious and pathetic proof of the odd use to which stage "business" may sometimes be put occurs in a story told some time ago by Mr. Barrett in the *Theatre*. The "Spider" in *The Silver King* had a peculiar whistle, with which he used to signal to his accomplices, and after a while this whistle was raised from the individual to the general and became the signal of the whole company at the Princess's and of all the companies touring in the provinces—a masonic as well as windy suspiration of forced breath.

Mr. Barrett says that it was whistled into the wondering ears of many a would-be sleeper in the country towns when the "boys" were going home and bidding each other good-night. It was whistled by Jack across the street to Tom as a "Good-morning;" by Harry to

Dick as a "Come here, I want you;" by Clem to Joe as a "Where are you?" And amongst others who acquired the art of rendering the signal to perfection was the pretty little son of two members of "Company K," a general favourite, who had the run of the theatre, and was simply the idol of his father and mother.

This little fellow would sometimes indulge his Bohemian instincts to the extent of breaking away from his parents' lodgings, bound for the theatre; and now and then he would be found amiably wandering and hopelessly lost, on which occasions he would announce that he was "Austin Arfur Loder," and "I'se lost myself and can't find my way home;" and to the question "Where is your home, my little man?" he would promptly and invariably reply, "Ze fee-a-ter."

This nomadic habit caused his parents some anxiety, but it was not considered serious until one day, in a quaint little town on the rockbound east coast of Scotland, "Austin Arfur" was missing too long for the peace of those who were so devoted to him.

During the course of the play one evening,

in which, by an odd coincidence, the father and mother were simulating the joys of parents who had recovered their lost children, the landlady called at the stage door to know if Master Austin was at the theatre. He was not, and the actor and actress had to finish their performance distracted with fear as to their missing child.

Hurrying from the theatre to their lodgings at the first possible moment, it was only to find no news of their boy. Their distress was terrible, and all night long search was kept up, some of the good-hearted fellows at the theatre foregoing their rest to help in the pathetic business.

When day broke, the agonised father and mother and a comrade in the company searched the cliffs by the sea shore, the mother hoping still to find that the little Austin had fallen asleep in some grassy glade, while the father feared the worst.

At last, weary and sick at heart, they were turning to retrace their steps and renew their search in the town, when, by some strange instinct, the actor gave the "Spider's Whistle."

A faint echo seemed to come to them from below. "Answer, Tom," said the comrade. "I can't," replied the father, overcome with emotion, while the mother screamed, "Austin! Austin! where are you?" The faint sound of the whistle was heard again, and in another moment the father was making his way down the face of the cliff at the risk of his own life, to the cave whence the sound seemed to proceed.

The tide was rising. Every moment meant the nearer approach of death; but despair gave the father a new strength, and at last, clinging, sliding, leaping, panting, breathless, his hands covered in blood, he was at the mouth of the cave, and his child was safe in his arms, saved by the "Spider's Whistle."

On December 6th, 1883, Mr. Barrett produced the remarkable play *Claudian*, by Messrs. W. G. Wills and Henry Herman, himself assuming the title *rôle*. The drama contained much that was noble in sentiment, and was superbly staged and admirably acted. It tells the story of the crime, punishment, and repentance of a pagan libertine, who, for the murder of a holy hermit who would have stood in the way of his unbridled passion, is condemned to perpetual youth, coupled with the doom of yearning to do good yet seeing all those whom he would bless cursed and blighted by the baleful influence which attends his every action. The prologue takes place in Byzantium, A.D. 362, and the play a century later.

Mr. Barrett's Claudian Andiates proved a fine study, picturesque and powerful to a degree. Whether as the handsome young patrician voluptuary of the Prologue, or the remorse-stricken man of the play, Mr. Barrett was admirable. His appearance was strikingly effective, his acting almost faultless. By a score of little touches he brought out the full significance of the story, and the classic dress of the period suited him to perfection. The earthquake tableau, where, in the midst of the ruined palace, Claudian poses in an attitude of horror and despair, was a scene not to be easily forgotten. Mr. Barrett's excellent elocution also stood him in good stead, and whether he was expressing the defiant voluptuousness of the patrician profligate, or the agony of the miserable, repentant man who, with a heart full of good intent, sees evil dog his footsteps everywhere, the actor's voice and gestures brought out the full force and significance of the text, and helped to bring about an unqualified success.

On May 22nd, 1884, Mr. Barrett produced a dainty and effective little piece, a tragedy in miniature, by Messrs. Henry Arthur Jones and Henry Herman, in which were sketched in dramatic form the episodes in the life of the ill-starred boy-poet Chatterton immediately preceding his pitiable death in the Brooke Street garret, blent skilfully with the love interest necessary to lend the story the element of romance requisite to ensure widespread popularity.

Gracefully, if now and then rhapsodically, written, Chatterton was an instant success. But this success was due in an even greater degree to the actor than to the authors. It would be scarcely too much to say that Mr. Barrett *was* "Chatterton," poet and play alike, for from first to last he overshadowed everybody else by the tenderness, pathos, and picturesqueness of his remarkable impersonation. He looked the handsome, harassed, weary, yet passionate and contemptuous boy-poet to the life, dowered with "the scorn of scorn, the hate of hate," jaded, starving, despairing, loving, to the bitter end of his few and stormy years.

The pride of Chatterton, his chivalrous love, his contempt for the dull, plodding, prosaic world, his passion for poetry, his mad ambition, were all indicated by Mr. Barrett as only genius could. By subtle gesture and splendidly versatile elocution the actor laid bare the very soul of the poet. As was said of Byron, "He made a pageant of his bleeding heart," but so delicately, and with such unerring tact, that he won for the mimic Chatterton a sympathy which the real poet sought in vain, even from posterity—usually so lavish when it is too late.

As a piece of delicate yet impassioned acting, Chatterton was a veritable artistic triumph. The admirable fashion in which Mr. Barrett declaimed the rather long-winded but elegantly written apostrophe to poetry remains a lucid memory with those who heard it; and the quickly following ecstasy and agony with which

MR. WILSON BARRETT AS HAMLET

he first finds Lady Mary's letter, offering him the love and fame and fortune he has craved so passionately, and all at once remembers that in his hopeless misery he has taken poison, and that the good news comes too late, was a marvellously rapid and convincing transition from rapture to despair, only equalled by the pathos of the death scene, which was a dramatic realisation of a beautiful and familiar picture.

Mr. Barrett's Hamlet was naturally the subject of much speculation, and the evening of October 16th, 1884, found an eager audience crowding every corner of the theatre. The grand simplicity of Shakespeare has too frequently been buried beneath a mountain of imaginary subtleties, and there has been no creation of Shakespeare's brain which has been the subject of so much pseudo-subtle speculation, and often absurdly unnecessary controversy, as Hamlet. The tendency has been to lay so much stress upon the character as a purely psychological study that the intense and passionate humanity of the young prince has been relegated to the background, as an aspect of the creation only worthy of secondary, if of any, serious consideration. Ridiculous controversies have raged with the virulence of theological discussions upon what it has been the cant to call the vexed question of Hamlet's real or assumed insanity, when a reasonable reading of Shakespeare's text must surely set the question at rest for ever.

It was a matter for congratulation that Mr. Barrett's Hamlet was so vividly instinct with human life, and with passions common to all humanity, that it became no longer a mere psychological study, to be critically dissected as a surgeon would dissect a corpse, but a living, breathing personality, a man with all the strength and weakness of manhood,—a noble nature weighed down with a heavy burden of grief and an onerous duty of revenge; but, for all that, one whose grief was as real, and commanded as genuine a sympathy, as the troubled career of some living person near and dear to our very selves.

Mr. Barrett's Hamlet was a young prince of noble nature, sorely tried by the conduct of his mother, and impelled by intense filial affection to avenge the foul murder of his father.

A very comprehensible character and condition this, and there is, very properly, no question about the sanity of Hamlet as represented by Mr. Barrett. By making it patent at once that Hamlet is no crack-brained prince, but a youth whose trouble is so heavy that it compels him to a course opposed to his natural kindliness, Mr. Barrett secured the immediate interest of his audience, and by emphasising consistently from beginning to end his intense love for his father, the new Hamlet compelled sympathy.

It was thus that Mr. Barrett instinctively took the surest road to popularity. His Hamlet was a man of like passions with ourselves, differing only in degree. Filial devotion, utter horror of a most foul crime, a painful sense of the burden laid upon his youth, changing what should be a period of joy into a time of plotting, and the agony of a mind racked by conflicting passions,—these were the notes upon which the new Hamlet played, and with such skill that his audience were at one with him from end to end. By making Hamlet comprehensible Mr. Barrett by no means made him commonplace, and although his impersonation was so thoroughly human and sympathetic as to be intelligible to the most unlettered of his audience, it still afforded ample material for study by the cultured and the critical.

From the moment of his impressive entrance, with the slow and measured step of sorrow, the one dull blot upon the boisterous gaiety of a semi-barbaric court, glittering with gold and colour—to the touching death, with the portrait of his well-loved father at his lips, the new Hamlet carried the audience with him in a creation at once emotionally and intellectually satisfying. Shakespeare, harassed by his learned commentators, has been compared to Actæon, worried to death with his own dogs. Mr. Barrett called off the dogs, and for that the countrymen of Shakespeare should be grateful.

It may be thought that the mere *physique* of such a character as the student-prince is a matter of comparatively little moment, but such is not by any means the case. To enjoy a representation of *Hamlet*, or any other play, it is essential that the audience should be in full sympathy with the prominent personages brought before them. The contemplation of a play should be one of the most perfect sources of æsthetic gratification, and this can only be when the senses are simultaneously pleased; when there is no discordant note in the chord which is to charm us out of ourselves. A coarse face may be wedded to a melodious voice, or a silver voice to a clumsy figure and uncouth gestures, and the result is that the bad neutralises the good.

Fortunately, in the Hamlet of Mr. Wilson Barrett the æsthetic harmony was complete. A perfect Hamlet should at least approach our ideal of the highest standard of physical and mental refinement. His mind should teem with cultured ideas, and his face and form and bearing coincide with the lofty tenor of his mind. The thoughts conceived by the student-prince and lover are of the highest, and the voice, the gesture, the movement in which these bright thoughts find expression should be too, in their way, of the most perfect that can be conceived. No harsh or vulgar accent should mar the sublimity of the sentiments which the young prince utters in his dire distress and innate nobility of mind; no clumsy gait should detract from the awe, the pathos, or the dignity of his bearing in the various life-scenes in which he is forced to take part; no *outré* fancy in the fashion of his apparel should distract the mind of his audience from the perfect comprehension of Shakespeare's magnificent creation. The words of the part should flow fittingly from the lips of the actor, whose every look and gesture should help us to realise the character which was so very real to Shakespeare, as he painted with a loving, lingering pen the portrait of one of the most human and pathetic figures in the world's dramatic literature.

Mr. Wilson Barrett fulfilled these conditions with a quite exceptional completeness. Physically he was an ideal Hamlet,—the handsome, weary face and boyish figure realising to the full the ideal portrait which the student of Shakespeare must inevitably have painted in his own mind. Voice, gesture, and movement were alike good, and in the details of dress the new Hamlet evidently spared no pains to be archæologically as well as æsthetically correct.

Herein may be found in a great degree the secret of his success. The intellect and the eye were at once satisfied, and a pleasant sense of completeness was felt by the most exacting and sensitive spectator. Mr. Barrett's Hamlet was not only the most human of modern times, but it gave us humanity at its best.

As an instance of the odd experiences, semi-humorous, semi-pathetic, which fall to the lot of actors more frequently than to ordinary humdrum folk, it may be told how, during the run of *Hamlet* at the Princess's Theatre, on arriving at his house " The Priory," North Bank, St. John's Wood, where George Eliot once lived, after the performance on a wretched winter's night, when the snow was several inches deep on the ground and in that half-frozen, half-thawed condition which is so intensely disagreeable, made still more unpleasant by a bitter north-east wind cutting into the very marrow of one's bones, Mr. Barrett saw leaning against the wall of the garden in the shadow the figure of a boy, apparently about twelve or fourteen years of age. Wondering what could have brought the lad there, the actor unlocked the garden door, and went into his cosy sitting-room, not without some qualms of conscience at his indifference to the shivering figure he had left outside. Consoling himself with the reflection that the boy was going home, and had merely stopped to see him get out of his brougham, Mr. Barrett tried rather ineffectually to dismiss the lad from his mind. On the following evening the weather was, if possible, still more unpleasant, but on arriving at the house there was the same little shivering figure in the same attitude—not courting observation in the least, but rather seeking the darkest shadow the wall afforded. This second apparition was more than Mr. Barrett could resist. He called to the boy to come to him, and a brisk dialogue ensued.

"What are you doing here, my lad?"

"Waiting to see you get out of your carriage, sir, that's all."

"Were you not here last night?"

"Yes, sir."

"But, my boy, you must be wretchedly cold and wet?"

"That's nothing if I can only see you, sir."

"What good can a hurried look at me do you?"

"It gives me courage to fight on, sir. I have heard of your early struggles, and how *you* conquered, and when I get down-hearted with my own troubles I always try to get a look at you, and so get fresh hope."

This *naïve* tribute, or diplomatic little bit of flattery, not unnaturally led Mr. Barrett to ask the boy to come indoors. Very reluctantly he was induced to do so, and, on getting him into the room, the actor had a good look at him. Short for his age, with large brown eyes, a refined face, close-cropped light brown hair, a small mouth, and very small hands and feet, the former blue with cold, the latter enclosed in a broken, down-at-heel pair of boots, through which the slush and snow had penetrated; he had on a pair of very frayed grey tweed trousers, and an Eton jacket; in his hand he nervously twirled a cloth cap.

"You must be very cold, come and warm yourself at the fire," said Mr. Barrett, drawing up a chair for the boy, determined to find out something of his history.

However, no persuasion could induce him to sit down, but there he stood at attention, waiting to be questioned. He would eat no supper, and said that his mother was awaiting him, and that *she* would have no supper.

This was enough for Mr. Barrett, who took up the cold joint and some bread, wrapping them in paper, with a bottle of wine, and gave them to him—with something else beside—bidding him go home, and wish his mother better times. Quite timidly the boy asked if Mr. Barrett could find some employment for him, and the actor promised to consult his business manager, Mr. John Cobbe, and told the lad to come on the following evening to the theatre. This he did. Mr. Barrett told him that he had talked the matter over with Mr. Cobbe, and had decided to try him as a messenger boy at first, leaving it to his own industry and perseverance to improve his position. The boy seemed deeply grateful, and Mr. Barrett sent for Mr. Cobbe.

"This is the lad I spoke to you about, Cobbe," said the actor-manager.

A quick, searching glance from Mr. Cobbe,

a queer look of suspense and anxiety from the boy. Then the usually placid Mr. Cobbe began slowly to colour crimson from the nape of his neck to the tip of his nose, and to Mr. Barrett's astonishment he turned to him, and said,—

" Mr. Barrett, this is not a boy at all, it's a girl!"

The figure in the jacket trembled a little, and the face grew as rosy red as Mr. Cobbe's, but not a word was spoken until Mr. Barrett broke the silence. " Is this true ?"

" No, sir, it is not."

" I'll swear to it," said Mr. Cobbe, "you came here some weeks ago ; you had written to Mr. Barrett for an engagement, and he deputed me to see you. You then wore a black dress, a sealskin jacket, and a black velvet hat. I told you there was nothing for you in the way of employment, and you went away."

"Are you quite sure of what you say ?' asked Mr. Barrett.

"Quite certain," replied his business-manager.

" It is not true!" still persisted the young

person. Here was a dilemma. Mr. Barrett could not doubt Mr. Cobbe.

The accused one trembled and blushed like any school-miss.

"I'm afraid Mr. Cobbe is right," said the actor at last, "and under the circumstances I must withdraw the offer I have made; if you are a girl you obviously cannot be a messenger boy, and there's an end of the arrangement."

"But he is wrong," this was accompanied by such a distinctly feminine stamp of the foot that all that Mr. Barrett could do was to say as gently as possible, "I am afraid he is right, and I can only wish you good-night, and advise you not to masquerade in this way in the future."

Then came the impulsive question, "Will you give me employment as a girl?"

Again the answer was compelled to be in the negative, and a flood of tears followed the refusal.

Mr. Barrett was sorry, but the Fates were not more inexorable.

One morning, taking up the daily paper, Mr. Barrett was reminded of the odd little figure in the snow, and the curious incident in which it was the principal actor in a strange fashion, by reading under the heading :—

"A STRANGE CASE,"

that "a young woman named —— was sentenced to six months' imprisonment for personating a boy!"

One of the most important dramatic events of 1885 took place on the 26th February at the Princess's Theatre, when Mr. Wilson Barrett gave to the world for the first time an unpublished as well as unacted drama by Bulwer Lytton—a notable addition to the best works of its author. *Junius* approaches in style rather to *Richelieu* than to other of Lord Lytton's works, making due allowance, of course, for the different periods with which the two plays are concerned. There is much nobility of sentiment couched in suitably noble diction; much worldly wisdom conveyed in aphorisms, and a great deal of fine writing in the play— fine in the best sense of the word, not the gilt and tinsel artificiality of *The Lady of Lyons*. Whether it is in depicting the half-savage sensuality and imperious self-indulgence of the ruling classes at a period when emperors were a law unto themselves, and government a tyrannic autocracy tempered by revolt and assassination, or whether it is in portraying the smouldering fires of rebellion in the hearts of dissatisfied patricians and an oppressed people, and contrasting the pure patriotism of a Junius with the unscrupulous and luxurious egotism of a Tarquin, the author is equally felicitous, equally vivid.

The Lucius Junius Brutus of Mr. Barrett consistently ignored the assumed foolishness of the patriot, and declined to emphasise the nickname Brutus bestowed upon him by the contemptuous Tarquin and his parasites, but which at the period when the drama opens had almost fulfilled its purpose, and was only necessary as a mask behind which, save before Tarquin and his following, Junius takes small pains to hide his real disposition. As Papinius says:—

> "Art thou so sure that Brutus is the clod
> Which Tarquin's scoff proclaims him? Hast thou ne'er
> Seen his lip writhe beneath its vacant smile?
> Seen his eye lighten from its leaden stare?

And heard beneath that hollow-sounding laugh
The slow, strong swell of a storm-laden soul?"

Here was the key to Mr. Barrett's reading of the part. The patriot entered, clothed in white robes, superbly handsome, with classic features, white hair clustering round a noble forehead, and every movement full of a dignity which gave the lie to Tarquin's brutal nickname —an ideal Junius, the "noblest Roman of them all." Alternately tender and bitterly scornful, gentle and indignant, intensely pitiful and passionately stirred to righteous vengeance culminating in the killing of Tarquin, Mr. Barrett lost no single one of the many opportunities of the part, and Junius proved an imposing and dignified figure, shining with greater lustre by the contrast of its classic simplicity and serenity with the gaudy, noisy, and effeminate parasites of the corrupt court of Tarquin.

The new play *Hoodman Blind*, by Messrs. Henry Arthur Jones and Wilson Barrett, produced at the Princess's Theatre on August 18th, 1885, was anticipated with considerable interest. It proved to be one more addition to the realistic-cum-sensational-cum-domestic dramas familiar to London playgoers since the inauguration of the new school of work by the production of *The Lights o' London*.

The manly, handsome fellow, wedded to a charming and confiding wife; the happy home blighted by the machinations of a well-dressed villain; the facile descent from solid comfort to squalid misery; the curiously sensational incidental episodes and odd acquaintances; the final frustration of the villain's wiles and restoration of happiness to the devoted but hoodwinked couple,—are they not written in the chronicles of the stage at any time since the loves and trials of Harold Armytage and Bess his wife, or Wilfred Denver and the faithful Nell, won our tears and took fast hold of our hearts?

The ingredients for that class of popular dramatic work being, apparently, not capable of much variety, it is well that they should be blent with discretion, and the authors of *Hoodman Blind* certainly concocted a palatable dish, although the cayenne was perhaps a little too self-assertive for the taste of the fastidious few. Sound judgment was shown in basing the play upon passions and motives common to all classes at all periods, and in exploding the fallacy that great cities enjoy a monopoly of vice.

The cruel wrong that might take place in a little old-world village such as Abbot's Creslow; the fierce passions that have play amongst scenes of Arcadian beauty; the love, the jealousy, the lying and slandering, the greed, the villainy that mar the lives of men and women, were shown to be as possible within the narrow limits of a hamlet as in the maze of monstrous London. And, by causing villainy to be enacted amid scenes of rural loveliness, the heinousness of crime was emphasised by force of contrast with its surroundings,—a perfectly legitimate method, utilised by the authors of *Hoodman Blind* with excellent effect.

The sketches of country life which preceded the realistic studies of squalid London had much in them of truth, the dialogue illustrating clearly the pettiness of rustic spite, the uncouth gambols of rustic humour, and the inordinate appetite of village folk for slanderous gossip. But the chattering village gossips, the garrulous village patriarch, the hysterically cheerful village brats, the sturdy, stolid rustics, had been seen so often that the advantage supposed to be conferred by the inclusion of "thirty-two speaking parts" in one play was not so obvious as might have been wished.

Literary merit was not wanting in the drama, and sometimes reached a high level, even when the eloquent diction clothed a conventional idea, but artistic self-restraint seemed lacking in some of the violent sentiments attributed alike to the villain and the hero of the piece. The treacherous Mark Lezzard expressed an amiable desire to "gnaw the heart" of the woman who would not marry him; while the hero, Jack Yeulett, in an extremity of provocation, talked ghoulishly of tearing a body from the grave, stamping upon the dead flesh, and casting the morsels over the earth.

Mr. Wilson Barrett was well fitted with the manly and picturesque *rôle* of Jack Yeulett, a young Bucks farmer, who, having sown his wild oats and married a charming and devoted wife, buckled to at a more profitable form of husbandry, not without success. But the

MR. WILSON BARRETT AS JACK YEULETT.

Nemesis of his old follies dogged his footsteps, and, just as he was happy in the love of his wife and five-year-old boy, a cloud hung over the simple tranquillity of his home, in the shape of the foreclosure of a mortgage, which meant the rending from him of house and land which had been in his family for generations, but possessed the compensating advantage of enabling him to deliver the first telling speech in the play.

Then blow followed blow. The faithful wife was made, by the arts of the villain, to appear false, and in a painful scene Jack Yeulett, a village Othello, flung her from him and left his home, with the wish that he may never look upon her face again. Then followed the usual sequence of trouble for both, until, after learning the truth by a miraculous interposition of "the long arm of coincidence," the hero dragged the villain to an elevated plateau in the centre of the village, extorted confession, then hurled the cowering wretch down amongst the clamouring people, who, with the quick, unreasoning fluctuation of a mob, stood eager to rend in pieces the man before whom but a day earlier they had cringed.

The play was admirably staged, excellently acted throughout, and Jack Yeulett was as striking, pathetic, heroic a figure as Mr. Barrett of all actors could make him, and both as actor and manager Mr. Barrett scored one more distinct success.

As part-author with Mr. Henry Arthur Jones of the romantic drama *The Lord Harry*, produced at the Princess's on the night of February 18th, 1886, Mr. Wilson Barrett was responsible for a not very novel but distinctly popular play, produced with richness and beauty, and affording him a dashing, gallant *rôle* such as he and his admirers loved. Fascinating and romantic as the era of Cavaliers and Roundheads, ruffling gallants and sour-visaged Puritans, had so often proved before, it was not surprising that the clever *collaborateurs* should fail to find much that was strikingly new to introduce, save a quite remarkable pinioning of a gaoler by a prisoner who rushes from behind the door of his cell, and an even more startling effect in a fight upon the roof of a nearly submerged cottage—an incident which would have been perilously suggestive of a nocturnal en-

MR. WILSON BARRETT AS THE LORD HARRY.

counter of tom-cats on the tiles, had it not been part of a scene of such rare beauty that irreverent criticism was stopped at the lips. Naturally the play turns upon the rival loves of Lord Harry Bendish, Royalist and ruffler, and a grim and treacherous Roundhead, Captain Ezra Promise, and the poetic idea of the gallant Cavalier's love for the memory of the tiny Puritan maiden who had given him a kiss many years before is very dainty and charming.

As the Lord Harry, Mr. Barrett had a part that suited his handsome presence and gallant bearing to perfection. The chivalrous speeches came not only trippingly but fittingly from his tongue. In his soldierly capacity Mr. Barrett was *bon camarade par excellence;* as a lover he was all that is ardent and tender, and as a Royalist the personification of chivalrous loyalty —a gallant manly figure throughout, carrying the play triumphantly to success upon his own broad shoulders.

A scene of intense enthusiasm marked the final fall of the curtain at the Princess's on the night of May 1st, 1886, and rarely had such a scene ampler justification. It was but fitting that a strikingly effective play, acted to perfection and superbly staged, should win such a success as was achieved by *Clito*, the new tragedy by Mr. Sydney Grundy.

There were those who, with ample faith in the managerial instinct of Mr. Wilson Barrett and the literary faculty of Mr. Grundy, hoped for rather than anticipated a success, when they heard that the new venture was to be a blank verse tragedy, with the action located in Athens in the year 400 B.C. But, as the event proved, the passions, follies, crimes, with which Clito was concerned were common to all time, and old as humanity itself; and this tragedy of ancient Greece was as full of moving interest as, and far richer in romance than, any modern drama of the sensational school, with which, indeed, it had nothing else in common, happily substituting a beauty and nobility of diction rare upon the stage of to-day for the sanguinary curses and platitudinising didactics of melodrama, and giving in its place loftily conceived tragedy, written with grace and vigour.

The story of Clito has all the simplicity of classic tragedy. A young Athenian sculptor,

Clito, pure and noble as a Greek Galahad, loathing the vicious luxury of the age, and fired with the wrongs of Athens, finds his adopted sister, Irene, in the power of a venal wretch employed by Helle, the mistress of the governor, Critias. He rescues Irene and joins a band of patriots, who plan the destruction of the palace and the sweeping away of Critias, Helle, and the vicious aristocrats by whom they are surrounded. Clito had often held the name of Helle up to scorn as the very synonym for all that was cruel and devilish, but Helle, at the instigation of the lustful Glaucias, seeks the sculptor in his studio, disguised, and practises all her arts upon him. Glaucias the cynic told her, "Art is immortal, but artists are mortal," and so it proved. Clito yielded without parley to the magic of Helle's wondrous beauty, and not only unwittingly betrayed his comrades by babbling to her of the plot, but, by visiting her at the palace, brought upon himself the odium of a traitor, only to find at last that the love for which he had sold himself, body and soul, was a lie. The vengeance of the patriots followed hard upon the heels of their betrayal, and fell first upon Helle, who had fled to Clito for protection, and then upon Clito himself, who died, stabbed to the heart, at the side of the dead Helle, the last word upon his lips—"Forgive!"

Here and there some slight anachronisms were evident, but for the most part the pathos and horror of the story were clothed in tender and terrible diction. The only humour which could be legitimately interwoven in a drama pitched in so high a key—satire of the keenest and the bitterest, the only humour possible in tragedy, and itself the very tragedy of humour—was introduced in discreet proportion, and the drama moved from first to last with firm, unfaltering step.

Mr. Wilson Barrett's impersonation of Clito was entirely admirable,—the alternations of human passion and exalted patriotism; the agonising struggle of a noble nature against the subtle and unflinching arts of an abandoned woman; the humiliation and remorse after the grievous lapse,—all were presented with Mr. Barrett's customary power and facility, and Clito became the centre of unflagging interest.

The Greek dress of the young Athenian sculptor was worn by Mr. Barrett with natural dignity and grace, and throughout the play he was a picturesque and poetic figure, fit hero for a tragedy of classic Greece.

Perhaps one of the most melodiously given as well as exquisitely written passages in the play was that in which Clito described his ideal woman :

> " A woman, fair,
> For it is woman's province to be fair,
> And yet whose beauty is her smallest grace:
> No mail-clad Amazon with helm and spear,—
> Her only shield her native innocence.
> The charm of gentleness is round her head,
> The light of truth is in her gentle eyes,
> Her garment the white robe of chastity :
> While Charity, of all the virtues Queen,
> Sits on her brow.
> Fearless in well-doing, in sorrow strong,
> Healer of wounds, affliction's minister,
> More good than pious, just a little blind
> To mortal weaknesses. A woman born,
> Affecting not to scorn a woman's fate ;
> At peace with destiny, her husband's crown.
> Cheerful of spirit—empress of her home ;
> In presence tender and in absence true :
> One who, when travelling life's common way,
> Glads every heart and brightens every eye :
> One in whose wake the beaten tracks appear,
> A little greener where her feet have trod '

The play was staged with a lavish magnificence rare even under Mr. Barrett's liberal management; the acting of Miss Eastlake as Helle was in some respects the finest thing she had ever done, and, as a whole, *Clito* was a completely worthy production and a distinct artistic success.

After an extended tour in America, where he received a cordial welcome, on the 22nd December, 1887, Mr. Barrett made his reappearance in London, and a crowded audience received him, within the walls of the Globe Theatre, with an enthusiasm which must have reminded him of old days at the Princess's, and certainly proved that his temporary absence had not dulled their cordial goodwill and admiration for him.

The new drama produced upon the occasion was from the pens of Mr. Barrett and Mr. G. R. Sims, and *The Golden Ladder*, as it was called, exhibited a type of stage hero new to the actor. The Rev. Frank Thornhill proved to be a muscular Christian of missionary experience, and distinctly a son of the Church militant—a fine, manly fellow of noble instincts, who gave early evidence of his generous nature by relieving the father of the girl he loved from threatened ruin, by the sacrifice of his own fortune. The heroine, not to be outdone in generosity, elected to marry Thornhill in his self-imposed poverty and share the hardships of life in Madagascar with him. After this came trouble upon trouble, in accordance with the habit of this class of drama to make its misery fertile after its kind, and a spell of poverty in Hampstead was followed by an agonising scene in Millbank, where the heroine was unjustly imprisoned for murder while her only child lay dying.

Mr. Barrett rarely looked better or acted with more force and pathos than in the exacting *rôle* of the Rev. Frank Thornhill. Manly, strong in body and mind, earnest and artistic throughout, he gave a picture of a noble-natured man fighting fortune bravely against fearful odds, with a sincerity and thoroughness which carried the audience with him, and secured an artistic success for a melodrama of too painful a tone to win enduring popularity.

A high-spirited, good-hearted, and altogether

lovable lad, to be presently transformed by events into the sterner stuff of triumphing and then sorrowing manhood, was the sort of character tolerably sure to appeal powerfully to Mr. Barrett's artistic sympathies, to gain the favour of an audience accustomed to see their favourite actor the central figure of stirring and romantic scenes, and further to win for its impersonator a great popular success. So it was not surprising that Mr. Hall Caine's powerful but rather sombre novel " The Deemster" should be adapted for the stage by the author and Mr. Wilson Barrett, and produced with complete success on May 17th, 1888, under the more attractive title *Ben-my-Chree*.

The Dan Mylrea was, of course, Mr. Wilson Barrett, and the *rôle* gave him many opportunities of displaying his versatility, of which he availed himself to the full. The impersonation was, in the earlier stages, so bright, breezy, lovable a piece of work, that the sympathy of the audience was secured at once, and, that achieved, Mr. Barrett could be trusted to do nothing to alienate it throughout the remainder of the play. The boyish debonair bearing in the first place, the sudden access of natural triumph over his defeated cousin, and then the anguish of discovering that the man is dead, were so forcibly, so naturally, conveyed, that the audience were carried out of themselves by the sheer strength and compelling realism of the actor. Mr. Barrett once more proved himself an artist *au bout des ongles* in Dan Mylrea, which must always rank with his most popular, picturesque, and well-thought-out creations.

On February 12th, 1889, Mr. Barrett appeared in *The Good Old Times*, a new drama written by Mr. Hall Caine and himself; but the result was not wholly satisfactory. As John Langley Mr. Barrett was robust and manly as ever, but the redundancy of dialogue, the presence of many improbabilities, and the falling-off from the dramatic excellence of *Ben-my-Chree*, were too apparent, and the play could not be added to the list of Mr. Barrett's successes. Of course there were moments when the actor's personal energy and charm rose superior to the comparatively unfavourable conditions of a too sensational melodrama; but, judged as a whole, *The Good Old*

Times failed to satisfy those who were familiar with the vastly better work previously done both by author and by actor.

On the night of February 28th, 1889, Mr. Barrett appeared at the Princess's in a drama of his own. Succeed or fail, he could say of *Nowadays : a Tale of the Turf*," " Alone I did it ! " No collaborator divided the honour or the responsibility. And *Nowadays*, happily, proved at least a tolerable success. The horse-loving British public, from the sporting butcher-boy with his shilling sweep to the noble Duke who plunges in five figures, might reasonably be counted upon to take some interest in a play in which all the action was made to revolve around a high-mettled racer ; and when, in addition to the equine interest, a considerable amount of human sentiment was introduced, a certain conventionality alike of character and central idea could easily be condoned.

But the play found its most interesting feature in the fact that for once Mr. Barrett flew in the face of nature, relegated romance to oblivion, discarded alike picturesquely " looped and windowed raggedness," classic toga, Cavalier plumes, the inky cloak, the Silver Regal hat of soft black felt with brim of subtly artistic curve, for the suit of rough grey frieze of a sturdy Yorkshireman, horsey and honest as a typical North-countryman should be.

And with the toga and the plumes went the highflown sentiment, the hairbreadth 'scapes, the heroic endurance of immeasurable wrong, the psychological subtlety, and the superhuman attributes of other days, for plain John Saxton was as homely, shrewd, big-hearted, obstinate a specimen of a downright manly man as Yorkshire itself could produce. The necessary pathos was provided by the presence of a well-loved daughter, who, yielding to the solicitation of the arch-villain of the story, not only marries him secretly, abandons her home, and aids him and his co-conspirators to steal and hide the Derby favourite, but, when a rescue party visits the Brixton stable to which the equine hero has been smuggled, very nearly shoots her father.

That Mr. Barrett could assume with so much success and so much force and realism the *rôle* of a grey-headed, rough-tongued old Yorkshireman proved, in a way peculiarly gratifying to his most discreet admirers, that he possessed the versatility indispensable to acting talent of the first order, and that although apparently doomed by nature to the perpetual enactment of handsome heroes of romantic drama, he could, on occasion, shine very effectively as one of the rough diamonds of humanity.

On December 4th, 1890, after a successful tour in America and the provinces, Mr. Barrett assumed the reins of management at his new London home, the New Olympic Theatre in Wych Street, built upon the site of the old building where, as Hood said of himself and his brother wits, they would

> " In the small Olympic pit sit, split,
> Laughing at Liston, while they quiz his phiz."

Mr. Barrett opened his new theatre with a drama by Mr. Victor Widnell and himself, called *The People's Idol.*

The play chosen for the inauguration of the new theatre proved to be a somewhat conventional type of drama, dealing rather superficially with the great question of "strikes" and the relations of capital and labour as they are understood or misunderstood to-day. In *The People's Idol* Mr. Barrett created the part of a certain well-born employer of labour, one Lawrence St. Aubrey, a young gentleman of most excellent presence and most tender sympathies, combined with an earnestness of purpose and a dogged resolution not to be cowed by threats, which redeemed the character from effeminacy. Tender as a woman with the unhappy souls who are reduced to misery by the strike, brave as an English gentleman should be when personal peril hems him in, a loyal and chivalrous lover, and a self-sacrificing elder brother to a selfish and weak lad who has got into a troublesome intrigue—there were many good points about Lawrence St. Aubrey, and these the actor did not fail to emphasise with all the resources of his melodious voice and admirably finished art; but the one strong incident in the play, the killing of the villain, Jim Stevens—agitator, drunkard, and "The People's Idol"—was marred originally by the sequent improbability of the ironmaster's intense remorse, which led him to shrink and shudder as though he had committed some dastardly crime, instead of at the worst killing a would-be murderer in self-defence. Mr. Barrett's acting was entirely good in this scene and its sequence, but the situation, though dramatically effective, was ethically false, and so, until it was in some degree amended, half its value went for nothing. The character of Lawrence St. Aubrey, contrasted sharply with that of the malignant Jim Stevens, was essentially one to strike the popular imagination, and the philanthropic sentiments put into his mouth were entirely in harmony with the manly, generous nature conceived by the authors; but for all that the effect produced was much less remarkable than that by such characters as Wilfred Denver in *The Silver King*, of which now and then faint echoes seemed to be recalled as *The People's Idol* unfolded its story. That Mr. Barrett made Lawrence St. Aubrey the cynosure of the scene whenever he was on the stage goes without saying, and no man on the boards could have created the *rôle* with more convincing realism. That London playgoers were glad indeed to see him permanently back amongst them was proved by a welcome so enthusiastic, so spontaneous, so affectionate, that it might have gladdened and touched the heart of any actor, as it obviously did that of Mr. Barrett, who was plainly moved when he found that during his temporary absence from the London stage he had not been forgotten by his admirers, who, on the contrary, vied with each other in the warmth of their welcome to an actor-manager who had given them so much worthy and brilliant work in the past.

Mr. Wilson Barrett at home in his charming house in Maresfield Gardens, South Hampstead, is just the same manly, frank, winning personality as on the stage. Full of pictures, books, and beautiful things, the house is essentially the home of an artist, and amongst other souvenirs of his own career, and of the profession which he loves so well, Mr. Barrett treasures a number of delightful letters from famous men, notably one from Mr. Ruskin, in which, writing of *Claudian*, the great Art critic says: "You know perfectly well, as all great artists do, that the thing is beautiful, and that you do it perfectly. I regret the extreme terror of it, but the admirable doing of what you intend doing, and the faithful co-operation of all your combination, and the exquisite scenery, gave me not only much more than delight at the time, but were a possession in memory of very great value. What a lovely thing it would be for you to play all the noble parts of Roman and Gothic history in a series of such plays. . . . These things, with scene-painting like that at the Princess's Theatre, might do more for Art teaching than all the galleries and professors in Christendom." Another letter, from Mr. Justin McCarthy, expresses the great pleasure which he found in the study of Mr. Barrett's *Hamlet,* "which explained much to him in a true light, and which will always remain in his memory with the few truly artistic performances it has been his good fortune to witness."

Another valued souvenir of one of his greatest successes is a handsome silver tankard, of Georgian design, grapes and vine leaves forming the decoration, and the lid being surmounted by a stag, presented to Mr. Barrett, with a pair of goblets, by the authors of *The Silver King*, and bearing the following inscription, "To our

Silver King, a token of our gratitude—a tribute of our admiration. Henry Arthur Jones and Henry Herman;" while on one goblet is inscribed, " Long Life to our Silver King," the other, " Health, Wealth, and Happiness to our Silver King."

Mr. Barrett's favourite part is Hamlet, and his theory of emotion in acting is interesting in view of the difference of opinion on this point. Mr. Barrett has said, " Tears come into my eyes unbidden when I am acting my best. With an effort I can repress them, but if I am not sufficiently in my part for them to come uncalled, no power of mine can bring them. . . . But mere feeling, unguided by art, is seldom, if ever, effective. Art without feeling is better than that, but feeling, with art, is better than both. The most sensitive organisation, coupled with the highest art, makes the greatest actor." Mr. Barrett has also asserted his belief that personal sorrows have influenced his acting for good.

After the comparatively brief run of *The People's Idol*, which for some reason or other failed to enlist the interest of the town, to the extent which might reasonably have been anticipated, Mr. Barrett commenced a series of revivals of his old successes, such as *The Silver King*, *The Lights o' London*, etc.; as well as giving some peculiarly interesting *matinées* of *The Lady of Lyons*, with himself as a gallant Claude Melnotte; and a revival of Kotzebue's sombre old play *The Stranger*, in which Mr. Barrett assumed the title *rôle* with considerable effect, and succeeded in proving that the human interest of the play was strong enough to counterbalance its old-fashioned flavour, and to compel sympathy even from the *blasés* audiences of to-day.

FROM A PHOTOGRAPH BY THE STEREOSCOPIC COMPANY.

Yours faithfully
Herb^t Beerbohm Tree
1890

Only the lines that sin and passion wear disfigure — sorrow and suffering, humbly borne, draw with an artists' pencil."
(Village Priest).

H. BEERBOHM TREE.

ORIGINALITY, subtlety, perfection of finish, and a quite remarkable versatility make Mr. Beerbohm Tree one of the most interesting figures of the stage of to-day.

He is a veritable chameleon. Alike in stage physique and in dramatic psychology he is constantly changing with absolute completeness and apparent absence of effort. The gods have been good to him, giving him just the physical and mental attributes of an ideal actor. Even his defects are helpful from the histrionic standpoint. Upon his thin colourless face he can paint just what picture he may need. Only the clear, glittering light blue eyes betray his identity.

Never has an actor possessed a more accommodating set of features. A master of the art of making-up, Mr. Tree assumes at will most widely diverse facial characteristics, nor do his other physical attributes lend themselves less kindly to the exigencies of his profession. A touch of the hare's foot, an artistic dishevelment of the hair, a cunning wrinkle in a coat, the tie of a bow, the angle of an eyebrow, the crook of a knee, the slope of a shoulder, and his audience may read rascal in the motions of his back and scoundrel in the supple-sliding knee; or he will make them recognise all the manly virtues by a well-padded frock-coat, the whimsicality of human nature in a wig, the pathos of a life in a bowed head, its villainy in a toss of the hand, its cynicism in a curl of the lip, its passion in a glance from his gleaming eyes.

Two remarkable instances of this rapid versatility, this absolute power of merging his own personality, both of body and mind, in the characters he assumes, were his impersonations of the starveling Gringoire, all fire and soul, and that huge hill of flesh and animality, Sir John Falstaff; and, on another occasion, the handsome, rattling hero of the comedietta *Six and Eightpence*, and the cringing, currish, treacherous Philip Dunkley in *Breaking a Butterfly*. In both these cases the characters assumed, with only the rising and falling of a curtain between them, were the very antitheses of each other, alike physically, intellectually, and morally, yet in each the actor was equally good, simply because he was no longer Beerbohm Tree, but the person whom for the moment he was representing.

The ideal actor should personate any type of character, within certain physical limits, with almost equal facility, yet the most versatile are apt to have certain classes of impersonation which suit them more completely than others. This is the case with Mr. Tree. While he has proved his power of running up and down the gamut of human passions, and of sounding the depths as well as floating on the shallows of human character, he has shone conspicuously in the delineation of refined, subtle, cynical villainy—not so much that of an Iago as of the modern version of Mephistopheles—a mocking, heartless devil, dressed by Poole and not unpopular in society.

Or, if there is a better than this best, it is when the villain is upon a somewhat lower social platform, and his intellectual cynicism is tinctured with positive brutality and accentuated by personal eccentricity.

From the days when as an amateur, and a member of the Irrationals, he made a name by his clever realisation of Achille Talma Dufard in *The First Night*, and other *rôles* in which he has since been seen upon the regular stage, Mr. Tree has sought every opportunity of putting his versatility to the test. The wider the gulf between a new and a preceding part, the more zestfully has he approached it. And when he has made an addition to his album of villains he has invariably introduced some bold, or preferably some subtle touch, which has given each new character unmistakable individuality.

Mr. Tree's first engagement was to play at the Town Hall, Hythe, and at the end of the first week he ran up to London, a little elated at the style in which he had played the two principal characters.

On the Monday morning he went to lunch with some friends, and, being of a convivial disposition, forgot until the last moment that he was pledged to appear in Hythe at 8 p.m. He rushed to Charing Cross just in time to see the tail lamp of the 4.30 crawling out of the station. There was another train at 4.55, a slow one, but there was nothing else to be done, so Mr. Tree wired to his manager:—
" Missed train. Coming by 4.55."

Then came three hours of slow torture. Mr. Tree used silvern eloquence to get the train "put along," but for all that he paced up and down the carriage like a caged lion—as no doubt he esteemed himself—and got out at a station before Hythe, taking a cab, which was in those days something of an extravagance, in order to save every possible moment.

As the clock struck eight the actor arrived at the Town Hall, to find a crowd round the door, reading, wide-eyed and grumbling, the following placard :—

> "IN CONSEQUENCE OF THE
> SEVERE INDISPOSITION
> OF
> MR. BEERBOHM TREE,
> THE PERFORMANCE IS
> UNAVOIDABLY POSTPONED
> UNTIL TUESDAY."

It appeared that the telegram had been sent, "Coming by 8.55," which was of course equivalent to not coming at all.

This little slip cost Mr. Tree a fine of five pounds—just one pound more than his weekly salary in those "early struggle" days.

It was during this first engagement, too, that he played the blind Colonel Challice in *Alone*, at Folkestone, and got immensely praised for a subtlety which even he himself had not suspected. He was very nervous in those days, and forgot his lines. To avoid an absolute breakdown, he agreed with the prompter that he would snap his fingers whenever he had lost his words. The curtain went up, and as soon as the blind Colonel appeared the finger-snapping became fast and furious. Next morning Mr. Tree found that the local critic praised his performance without stint, complimenting him particularly on having mastered the habits of the blind so thoroughly, "even down to the nervous twitching of the fingers" (the snapping for the prompter's help), and "the listening for the falling leaf" (Mr. Tree's eagerness to catch the prompter's voice), "as though loss of sight made hearing more dear to him."

At the early stages of his career Mr. Beerbohm Tree was the subject of much friendly interest amongst those who recognised in the new recruit one of the coming leaders of the mimic world behind the footlights, and in some cases this personal goodwill was shown in out-of-the-way fashion.

It was on the occasion of his first appearance in Dublin that a gentleman of Irish nationality proposed his health at a dinner in eulogistic terms, and subsequently took the opportunity of administering a few words of friendly counsel, punctuated by hiccoughs.

Drawing Mr. Tree aside in the smoking-room, he said with the abnormal gravity of incipient inebriety: "There's one rock, my dear boy, you must avoid. So many of you go to wreck on it. Drink, my boy, I mean. Drink! *What'll you take?*"

It is just about ten years since "the gentleman with the peculiar name," as one of the judges called Mr. Tree, began to attract the attention of those critical astronomers whose business it is to watch the theatrical firmament for the dawning of new stars, and to chronicle the movements of known luminaries. In May 1880 Mr. Tree's presentment of Monte Prade in Miss Geneviève Ward's production of Emile Augier's *L'Aventurière*, at the Prince of Wales's Theatre, impressed the critics and surprised the public by evidence of unsuspected power; and in June of the same year, playing at the same theatre in *Forget-me-not*, to Miss Geneviève Ward's wonderful Stéphanie de Mohrivart, he scored heavily in the minor part of the susceptible Prince Malleotti, his *finesse*, the delicacy of touch with which he gave the smallest detail a distinct value, and his obvious power of appreciating the inner essence of a character instead of merely treating it from the outside by means of emphasised peculiarities or strongly-marked idiosyncrasies, causing the more discriminating of his critics to welcome an actor of promise, and to anticipate his future work with more than common interest.

In July, at an Imperial *matinée*, his Sir Andrew Aguecheek in *Twelfth Night* gave the public their first taste of his quality as an exponent of Shakespearean humour, and was voted *impayable*, his extreme height and slimness fitting him so well physically for the representation of that "very yard-measure of a man"—the most striking contrast conceivable to his portly Falstaff of later years. Other clever studies led up to his famous impersonation of that physically limp, but mentally acute humbug, the "Professor of the Beautiful in Art," Lambert Streyke, in *The Colonel*, at the Prince of Wales's Theatre in 1881.

That Mr. Tree achieved success in parts differing so widely, and while his stage experience was as yet limited, was due to certain principles which he has held without wavering from the days of his obscurity to these of his brilliant success, and to that affinity to the stage which he considers absolutely essential. Mr. Tree's dicta upon these points are interesting for the side-lights which they throw upon his career.

Some time ago Mr. Tree expressed the following opinions:—" I consider a distinct attraction to and sympathy with the stage absolutely essential to success. And not, mind you, merely the attraction which leads men and women to go on the stage just to show themselves, or their dresses. I mean a thorough liking for their work, which will enable them to face the inevitable difficulties—for the work is often stone-breaking and heart-breaking. . . . As to genuine qualifications, I should say that a man should have a respectable education— especially a social education, which is, perhaps, of more value on the stage than a mere academical training. Then he should have this affinity or enthusiasm for his art—without it all is barren. That, and a knowledge of men and manners, are the first essentials. I would add, too, a capacity for hard work, and a determination, at all times and in all places, to do one's very best. There must be no 'playing down' to the intelligence of an audience—I detest the phrase! It is not the public who are wanting in intelligence. Give them credit for a capacity for appreciating all that you can give them, and give them of your best. No one who is an artist is content to put out his second-best. Indeed, he has no second-best; he does all he can—always. Audiences soon learn if a man plays as it were with his tongue in his cheek."

With regard to imaginary qualifications of aspirants to histrionic honours, Mr. Tree tells a capital story. A young fellow came to him and asked him to obtain a footing for him on the stage. "'What are your qualifications?' I asked him," says Mr. Tree, adding, "Imagine my position when he replied: 'Well, you see, I've got something wrong in my inside which interferes with my bicycling, and so I thought I'd go on the stage.' And," says Mr. Tree, "he went on, but not through me. He got on the boards as a banner-bearer. I afterwards ran against him by accident. He was still carrying a banner. Yes, and still had something wrong in his inside."

In May 1882 Mr. Tree found an impersonation which afforded him scope for his peculiar qualities in Mr. Herbert Gardner's drama *Time will Tell*, in which he played Count Czernocski, eliciting the opinion that as an instance of keen, incisive, discriminating character it was the best thing yet placed to his credit, original and highly finished. In this *rôle*, too, Mr. Tree's exceptional talent in making up was also the subject of comment, a clever bald patch on his wig being quite a touch of art, and the whole presentment of a cool, familiar, insinuating rascal being finished in every detail.

In September 1882 a new departure was made as Solon Trippetow, in that amusing piece *Miss Muffet*, by James Albery, at the Criterion, in which Mr. Tree displayed his characteristic thoroughness almost to excess, getting too much in earnest towards the end. As a critic said at the time, his assumption of gravity when lecturing his "awful dad" or admonishing his youthful mamma was full of the most genuine fun, but Solon Trippetow is most sublime when most ridiculous, and to make him too serious spoils the effect of a very original part. In November of the same year Mr. Tree figured conspicuously in Arthur Matthison's little piece *Brave*

Hearts as a poverty-stricken and eccentric French marquis; and on March 14th, 1883, we find him at the Olympic, a grotesque, wild, eccentric figure, Jabez Green, a half-cracked country lad, a sort of rustic Barnaby Rudge, in Mr. Robert Buchanan's *Stormbeaten*, the dramatic version of his story, "God and the Man." In this small part the instinct of the actor contrived to find material to work with, and the shambling, tripping figure, simple face and high-pitched

MR. H. BEERBOHM TREE AS PRINCE BOROWSKI, IN "THE GLASS OF FASHION."

voice, now and then cracking into falsetto, made the character one of those which stand out clearly in the memory. In March one more phase of the actor's talent was shown in Lord Boodle, the typical aristocrat in Mr. Hamilton Aïdé's comedy *A Great Catch*, at the Olympic Theatre, when it was said, " Mr. Beerbohm Tree, if laughter may be accepted as a fair criticism, achieved the greatest success."

It was on September 8th, 1883, that Mr. Tree created the part of which it may perhaps be said that it was so distinctive, so finished in the smallest detail, that it identified the actor once and for all time with the realisation of a type of polished foreign rascal which he has made peculiarly his own. This *rôle*, the forbear of quite a family of villains of a somewhat similar stamp, was that of Prince Borowski, in Mr. Sydney Grundy's smart comedy, *The Glass of Fashion*, produced at the Globe Theatre. The make-up was a study. The little forked beard, the meagre moustache daintily pointed, the affectation of militarism indicated by the broad trouser-stripe of braid, the carefully arranged hair and expanse of snowy shirt-front,—all were admirable, all helped the illusion and intensified the distinctiveness of the character. The mingled suavity and ferocity, the supreme selfishness and utter lack of scruple, the innate blackguardism forcing itself from time to time through the veneer of good breeding—all these were elements which were to be nurtured and cultivated, and to reappear in after days in various forms, anglicised in a Sir Mervyn Ferrand, exaggerated to some extent in a Slowitz, and with all the exotic rascaldom well to the fore in a Paolo Macari, a Prince Zabouroff, a Baron Hartfeld, and a Luversan.

Following the subtle, microscopic study of Borowski, successes came thick and fast. It was on May 20th, 1884, in the dramatised version of Hugh Conway's story "Called Back," that Mr. Tree clinched his reputation at one stroke by the creation of Paolo Macari,—a figure so picturesque, so superbly, superhumanly cynical, so consistent in every gesture, every glance, every accent and cadence of the voice, that each added something to the picture, and not one could have been spared without damage to its complete and convincing realism. It was not only with his cunning tongue and in his fascinating broken English that Macari spoke: his eyes, his supple figure, his cigarette, his moustache, the coat upon his back and the hat upon his head—were all eloquent. The self-indulgent indolence which is the frequent accompaniment, and often the direct cause, of craftiness, was indicated in a score of delicate touches, and Macari, gliding or swaggering, as occasion needed, about the stage, was the incarnation of that cynical proverb of his country which says that one has not learned how to live until one has learned how to dissemble.

But intervening between these creations were two strangely different types, both impersonated by Mr. Tree at the Prince of Wales's Theatre, on March 3rd and 29th, 1884, and differing as widely as the Poles: Philip Dunkley, the reptile banker's clerk, a red-haired invertebrate animal akin to Uriah Heep, in Messrs. Herman and Jones's version of Ibsen's play *Nora*, called *Breaking a Butterfly;* and the Rev. Robert Spalding, simplest, funniest, and mildest of curates, in Mr. W. F. Hawtrey's adaptation of Von Moser's farce *Der Bibliothekar, The Private Secretary*. The inventiveness, the apt appreciation of all that may be made out of or put into a part, the fertility of resource and quick-witted apprehension of possible additions so characteristic of Mr. Tree, now stood him in good stead. Mr. Spalding, with his lisp, his drawl, his perpetual cold in the head, his bandbox, umbrella, and goloshes, his blue ribbon, bag of buns, and bottle of milk, his guileless simplicity and childlike credulity, his dislike of London, and his physical and intellectual limpness, was a remarkable creation; and if the author provided a promising skeleton, it was the actor who largely clothed it with flesh and blood, and gave it much of its whimsical, grotesque personality.

It was the actor to whom such telling touches as the introduction of a bottle of milk and such catching phrases as: "I don't like London!" and "D'you know?" were due, while the blue ribbon in the button-hole was an inspiration at so late a moment that there was no time to procure a piece of actual ribbon before the first appearance of the Rev. Robert, and Mr. Tree's button-hole token of temperance was due, not to the draper, but to the scene-painter, whose colour was still wet upon the actor's coat when the curtain went up.

The curious compound of clerical complacency and natural imbecility of the Rev. Robert Spalding made him quite one of the funniest figures of the modern stage. The sleek fair hair and pale face, the incurable angularity of mind and body, the shortness and skimpiness of the black trousers and the length of fluttering skirt to the shiny black coat, the soft felt hat and the expansive umbrella, were all admirably consistent,—so consistent that it would have been difficult to imagine the man with any differing detail of dress, manner, or make-up. It was one harmonious and exquisitely funny whole, and proved that Mr. Tree was as much at home in grotesque characterisation and farcical comedy as in *rôles* demanding subtler treatment, and that he could produce bold effects with a broad brush as easily and as surely as the delicate half-tones which lent such distinction to characters demanding the touch of the miniaturist rather than that of the scene-painter.

From Macari to Joseph Surface is a far cry, but Mr. Tree proved himself to the full as fascinating a rascal in the satin coat and lace ruffles of an eighteenth-century comedy as in the more prosaic clothes of a villain of to-day, and walked in stately fashion through the scenes of the *School for Scandal*, sleek and suave,—

> "Soft smiling and demurely looking down,
> But hid the dagger underneath the gown."

His Joseph Surface was admirable, and once more the individuality of the actor was reflected in his impersonation, and he rendered one point in the play more reasonable by making Joseph better looking, better dressed, and better mannered than convention warranted—thus showing a wholesome disregard of stage traditions fully justifiable in the case of an actor strong enough to trust to his own conception of a character. By this innovation in the matter of make-up and dress, Mr. Tree made Joseph's illusion as to Lady Teazle's supposed *tendresse* for him intelligible; and by his quiet, convincing acting, Joseph Surface became an interesting study instead of the transparent humbug which he may so easily become in convention-tied or common-place hands.

It was on February 10th, 1885, that Mr. Tree appeared as the man of sentiment, and in September of the same year, and on the same stage, he added a remarkable creation to his gallery of aristocratic villains. In Sir Mervyn Ferrand, the most picturesque figure in Messrs. Comyns Carr and Hugh Conway's daring drama, *Dark Days*, Mr. Tree excelled himself. Melodramatic, ultra-sensational, verging at times perilously near to the grotesque, the play was admirably acted by others, notably Mr. Robert Pateman, as well as by Mr. Tree, but it is Sir Mervyn Ferrand who lingers in the memory, clear-cut as a cameo, and as enduring.

In the dramatic version of *Dark Days* two characters were introduced, and one, which was the merest sketch in the story, though, be it said, a sketch by a master-hand, was filled in with such ability that it became one of the most striking and interesting of the *dramatis personæ*. From being a mere *silhouette*, Sir Mervyn Ferrand became a study, the details of which were drawn with the fidelity of a Gerard Douw. In the story we have simply a suggestion of a villain ; in the play we have villainy incarnate.

MR. H. BEERBOHM TREE AS SIR MERVYN FERRAND.

The character was too promising a creation, though by no means a novel one, to be lost, and a sound discretion was shown in throwing back the action in the drama, painting the heartless life of the *blasé roué* in vivid colours, and at the same time relieving to some extent the sombre tone of the play by the light but cruel cynicism of the man of the world. The scenes in which Sir Mervyn Ferrand figured were among the finest in the play, owing in no small measure to the exquisite refinement and subtlety with which Mr. Beerbohm Tree impersonated a character of the class in which he is seen at his best. The assumed *nonchalance* of Sir Mervyn Ferrand, his airy *persiflage*, the curiously clever cynicism which by its apparent frankness disarms suspicion, the polished manner, the perfect refinement, and beneath them all the ever-present, hardly-veiled brutality,— all these were indicated by Mr. Tree as only an actor gifted with something more than mere talent could suggest them.

The new year provided Mr. Tree with an opportunity of adding to the villains of the stage a polished, patrician voluptuary, venerable in age but in nothing else, vicious with all the callous brutality of senility, a mirror of manner and a miracle of mercilessness,—the most repulsive yet interesting figure in a powerful but painful play. Admirably acted, Mr. Maurice Barrymore's sombre tragedy *Nadjezda*, produced at the Haymarket on January 2nd, 1886, failed to please the public for obvious reasons. Written with nervous force, the incident around which everything else revolved was too revolting for the work to hold the stage. But Zabouroff remains as fresh in the recollection of those who saw it as if only days had passed since the be-furred, aristocratic old libertine tottered about the stage, made his vile bargain, won his evil way, and then repudiated his word of honour like the veriest cad. Exquisitely dressed, perfectly groomed, with all the affectations of youth and the morbid viciousness of age, daintily gloved as a *demi-mondaine*, perfumed and powdered, false on the surface as he was at heart, Prince Zabouroff was the incarnation of aristocratic vice at its worst—accustomed to will and to have, contemptuously ignoring the necessity of keeping a pledged word to the common people, cool and conscienceless, unprincipled and unsparing of man or woman, false as dicers' oaths and cruel as the grave,—a libel on humanity, yet a libel for which truth might be pleaded in justification.

In February of the same year Mr. Tree appeared in two very different parts with success, although as Herr Slowitz, in Mr. B. C. Stephenson's *A Woman of the World*, his make-up and his conception of the part were a little exaggerated, and showed a tendency to lapse into caricature. Yet the humour of the impersonation was extreme, and there were enough clever touches in it to impel a critic to write of it : " Mr. Beerbohm Tree, as the tone-poet, added another brilliant figure to his gallery of eccentrics. His manipulation of his inky mop of hair—a reminiscence of Rubinstein —was simply superb, and his German accent was by far the best and most consistent I remember to have heard. His performance as a whole was a piece of admirable comedy, with just the legitimate dash of caricature."

It was in the same month Mr. Tree essayed

with success the part of the amorous Cheviot Hill, in Mr. W. S. Gilbert's cynical play *Engaged*.

In Sir Charles Young's powerful drama *Jim the Penman*, produced at the Haymarket on April 3rd, 1886, Mr. Tree once more had one of the parts which fitted him like a glove, —that of a German rascal, a financial swindler and trickster, Baron Hartfeld, whose half-bald wig, hooked nose, and black whiskers revealed at a glance the born schemer and impudent adventurer, without being either unnatural or conventional. In this *rôle*, too, the perfect werman accent of which Mr. Tree is master Gas assumed with admirable effect, and the presentment was full of quiet humour and convincing in its realism. As a type of adventurer such as may be found in shady offices round about Capel Court, Baron Hartfeld was *impayable*, and his Hebrew extraction was indicated without vulgar exaggeration.

During his appearance in *Jim the Penman*, Mr. Tree had a very amusing, if rather embarrassing, experience on the railway.

He had been down to Oxford, to play Iago

with Mr. Benson's company at a *matinée*, calculating that by dressing and making-up as Baron Hartfeld in the train he would reach the Haymarket just in time to prevent a stage wait.

But the Oxford performance was late, and Mr. Tree only just caught his train to London by throwing an ulster over his Iago dress and bolting for the station. Arrived there, he tipped the guard and got a compartment to himself. So far, good. By the first stoppage the Iago beard was off, and Mr. Tree bore the appearance of an ordinary English gentleman, to the obvious mystification of the guard, who looked in as he passed along the platform, stared, grunted, but ended at that. But when the time came for taking tickets, another metamorphosis had taken place. The Hartfeld wig, whiskers, and, above all, the Hartfeld nose, had been assumed, and when the hawk-like and forbidding face loomed out of the growing shadows in answer to the cry of "Tickets!" the suspicion of the guard was thoroughly roused.

And now, to cap it all, Mr. Tree had lost his ticket. This was the last straw, and with ominous severity the guard said sharply, "Lost it? I dessay! *Come! take off that nose! We know your sort!*" and it was only by the application of liberal largesse that the Haymarket audience was not kept waiting while the "three single gentlemen rolled into one" underwent the ordeal of being marched off in custody. And Mr. Tree is convinced that in his secret conscience that guard fully believes to this day that he aided and abetted in the escape of some desperate criminal.

In January 1887 Mr. Tree was an interesting study as Stephen Cudlip, the villain in Mr. Jones's drama *Hard Hit*, and April of the same year gave him an opportunity of adding to his *répertoire* a creation of a quite new kind, and upon this occasion he so excelled as a master of the art of self-effacement that it was not until he had strolled leisurely from the back of the stage to the footlights that the audience penetrated his wonderful make-up, and recognised, with a roar of applause, in the wily old chief of Russian police, Paul Demetrius, the personality of the young actor-manager. The success of

Mr. Outram Tristram's play *The Red Lamp*, produced at the Haymarket on April 20th, was unquestionably due to a very large extent to Mr. Tree's impersonation of the Chief of the Police. Made-up as a florid, leisurely, white-haired, stealthy old man, the physique, not fat, but ample; the baggy, ill-fitting dress suit; the fingers, diamond-ringed, ready for instant bribery; the humouring, tolerant tone, as of one whose ripe experience by no means inclined him to be hard upon human weaknesses; the sudden, swift leap into vivid life, with every sense alert to detect the enemies of the Czar; the inimitable banter with the venal little French baggage of a maid, so delightfully played by Miss Rosina Filippi,—all were perfect, and proved that the subtler the methods demanded, the more delicate the by-play, the more minute the indications of character, the more completely could Mr. Tree rise to the occasion. It is sufficiently easy to conceive a Demetrius who should have been simply commonplace and conventional, or who, escaping the Scylla of dulness, would have been wrecked on the Charybdis of caricature, and have so coarsened and vulgarised the part as to reduce the drama to the level of ordinary sensationalism, and render the bribery scene with the maid impossible,—thus robbing the stage of a perfectly irresistible bit of comedy.

And here it is worth remarking that although Mr. Tree is naturally the central figure of the dramas in which he appears it is often as much by what he puts into a part as by what he finds there, and that he has the excellent taste to content himself, when occasion seems to demand it, with a minor *rôle* in the plays which he produces, and thus prove that the actor-manager system is by no means synonymous with the old stock-company idea of "stars and sticks."

And upon this actor-manager system, Mr. Tree holds strong opinions. Replying to the attack made upon it, and other alleged abuses of the stage, by Mr. Oswald Crawfurd, Mr. Tree not only proved that he was well qualified to defend his position, but expressed views upon the stage of to-day full of shrewd sense and not lacking in humour.

Without running into the extreme of optimism,

Mr. Tree maintains that the drama is to-day as vital a factor in the life of the nation as it has been in any period of our history, and of all the arts, he says, it is perhaps the most popular. Whether this popularity is due to its inherent healthiness or to the degradation of public taste, to which managers have attempted to pander, is, he admits, debatable ; but while many stupid plays succeed, good plays do not meet with failure if worthily presented. Mr. Crawfurd attributes the present alleged degradation of the stage to four main causes : (1) mixed audiences ; (2) the apathy of the educated portion of these audiences ; (3) long runs; and (4) the actor-manager system. As to the first of these "causes," Mr. Crawfurd's "kid-gloved contempt for the 'gods,'" says Mr. Tree, shows that he has no sympathy with that wider influence of the theatre which is "beyond the mere pedantry of literature." The theatre should be regarded as a benefactor of the community at large. That art is best which is broadest, and it is the truest art which appeals equally to the simple and the scientific, —that which the man of genius would recognise and the coster would applaud. "What play," asks Mr. Tree, "has failed (with the public) from being too high in aim, too true in sentiment, too lofty in thought?" With regard to long runs, these are, in a sense, detrimental to artistic development. But if long runs were not to be, how could the author afford to devote the time and care to his work, and the manager be enabled to give the necessary labour to rehearsals, and the necessary capital for mounting?

As to the actor-manager system,—the pestilence which casts its withering blight on the fair flower of our art, which consigns the genius of the actor to a garret, and that of the author to the despair of a magazine article,—if actor-managers occasionally usurp positions to which their talents have not entitled them, the uncompromising common-sense of the box-office will speak with no uncertain voice, and the usurper will fall a victim to the fanaticism of his self-worship. Then, as to the mounting. The genius of Wagner disdained neither the art of the scene-painter nor the research of the archæologist. Yet, for the recognition of the more exacting artistic demands of the public, our managers are denounced as Goths and Vandals.

Mr. Tree argues also that nearly all the plays that remain favourites with the public contain what Mr. Crawfurd would call actor-manager parts. As to the establishment of theatres on "joint-stock principles," "reason pales, common-sense reels, and satire is dumb in face of such a proposition." The tendency at present, he says, is rather towards state-hampered instead of state-aided theatres. If the interference of "our grandmother the State" is a questionable blessing, it is surely not unreasonable, he adds, to protest against the tyranny of "our mother-in-law the County Council," whose absurd pretensions to take over the entire control of the theatres will, it is to be hoped, be consigned to "the dust-heap of oblivion along with the stucco statues and crinoline classics of the early Victorian Era."

On September 15th, 1887, Mr. Tree made a notable addition to his creations, as Gringoire in *The Ballad-monger*, Messrs. W. H. Pollock and Walter Besant's version of Theodore de

Banville's play of that name. The starved, half-crazy revolutionary poet, lean of frame, clad in picturesque rags, with his heart fired by a passion for an unattainable woman and his lips inspired by love of the people, suited Mr. Tree's intense, nervous style to perfection. With his alternations of wild, half-hysterical rhapsody, passionate denunciation, and fierce contempt, Gringoire is a remarkable personality, and in Mr. Tree's hands every phase of the man was made to yield its fullest value. Despair and hope, eager love-pleading and fierce denunciation of kingly vice; the bitter sarcasm in which were voiced the hatred of a disaffected people; the passionate abandonment of love-rhapsodies and the scathing satire of " King Rope," hurled in half-drunken frenzy at the head of the wily Louis,—all the passion and pathos of a poet's breaking heart and a people's dumb despair were embodied in this impersonation, which was followed in January 1888 by a character of a quite new type—all simple humanity, large-hearted, gentle, full of manly dignity, quiet humour, pure pathos, and an almost womanly tenderness.

This new and beautiful study was Heinrich Borgfeldt, in Mr. Buchanan's play, *Partners*, an adaptation of Alphonse Daudet's story " Fremont Jeune et Risler Aîné," produced at the Haymarket on January 5th, 1888. In this all the villainy, craft, passion, slipped away, and in their place the actor gave us a delightful picture of humanity at its best, but subject, as such types often are, to being tricked, duped, dishonoured, by a trusted friend. A simple-minded merchant, the soul of honour, happy in the affection of his wife and worshipping his little daughter ; content with shabby clothes and simple pleasures, coming from his office to the pure pleasures of domesticity,—nothing could be more touching, more tender, more true than the Heinrich Borgfeldt of Mr. Tree. The charming broken English, the exquisite touches by which his love for wife and child were suggested, the make-up, from the thin greyish hair to the ill-cut trousers and clumsy boots, were all as artistic as could be, and, too, Mr. Tree displayed in this *rôle* the truest art of all, that of self-restraint. Beautiful and touching as were the scenes in which the great love that was his life beamed upon wife and child; whimsical and winning as was the humorous catechising of his little girl as she perched upon his knee while he enjoyed his long-stemmed pipe with the painted china bowl from the Fatherland,—it was in the office scene, when the foul treachery of his young partner is made known to him, that Mr. Tree was really great. It was a superb example of self-control, a triumph of quiet power.

With brief spells of varied effort, we arrive at Mr. Tree's next striking impersonation, on May 31st, 1888, when he appeared as Narcisse Rameau in Messrs. W. G. Wills and Sydney Grundy's romantic play *The Pompadour*, adapted from Diderot's *Neveu de Rameau*. This creation belonged to the same school as Gringoire, but with his keen perception of minutiæ, Mr. Tree succeeded in giving it distinct individuality. Again the half-starved man of the people was sharply, almost painfully, contrasted with royal luxury and extravagance; but in the case of Narcisse Rameau it is not the love of the people, but love for a lost wife which is the paramount passion. The vagrant with so soft a heart and so tender a remembrance of the woman he loves—so tireless in his search, so pathetic when he discovers his lost wife in the king's mistress—was splendidly drawn; and amid all the vivid colour and restless movement of the gay crowds of courtiers and favourites of Louis Bien-aimé, it was the vagabond Narcisse of the meagre figure and wild face who dominated the stage.

Another turn of the kaleidoscope and we find Mr. Tree assuming one more distinctly fresh type of character in Mr. Wilding, alias "Captain Swift," in Mr. C. Haddon Chambers's drama of that name, first produced at a Haymarket *matinée* on June 20th, and put into the evening bill on September 1st, 1888. Bushranger and desperado, yet not without that "soul of good" which is to be found even in things evil; with the refinement and polish of a man of the world, and the compelling power which such qualities in combination could alone give, Mr. Wilding is a curious study, not without the power of winning sympathy, and with a cool imperturbable self-possession which is in itself fascinating. The chord of pathos is struck with no uncertain touch in the relations of the man and his mother, who, married and moving in society respectable to the verge of Grundyism, has lost sight of this son,—the fruit of an unhappy passion in her youth,—but has always had her life shadowed by her secret. There were moments when Mr. Tree was seen to immense advantage,—notably when he turned with fierce contempt upon the cringing servant who discovers his identity and tries to blackmail him, and again when, after recognising him as her son, his mother pleaded that he would speak "one word of love" to her, and he answered her with a sob, half of fierce resentment, half of natural pity, and the pathetic cry, "You never taught me how!"

As a psychological study, this impersonation was of extreme interest. The sense of something lacking, of some inevitable and painful difference between himself and others, breeding a despairing defiance of society, a wild joy in preying upon respectability, a morbid sensitiveness in resenting a secret shame, were indicated by the actor in a score of subtle ways. The dual nature in man and the desperate mischief bred by a sense of social alienation were excellently shown, and the strength and pathos of the part brought out to the last degree.

Insanity, or monomania, is a tempting subject to any actor with a special talent for the delineation of psychological phenomena, and it is not surprising that Mr. Tree approached the *rôle* of Matthew Ruddock, in Mr. H. A. Jones's play *Wealth*, produced at the Haymarket on April 27th, 1889, with something like eagerness, and there were many points and moments in it of real value. The character of the old manufacturer, consumed with a passion for money-making, devoted to his daughter but more devoted to his ducats, was a study in mental as well as moral pathology, and, so conditioned, Mr. Tree was of course admirable. Now and then the situations called for certain physical powers which he does not possess, but in the general outline of the character nothing was blurred or indistinct, and the mental troubles involved in the double illusions of wealth and penury were rendered with extreme realism and *finesse*. In the opinion of an able critic, Mr. Tree, with his refined and delicately constructive rather than impetuous talent, was misplaced in such a part. But for all that there were great moments in the play; for instance, Matthew Ruddock's reading of the little letter written by his daughter when a little child, which was perfect in its unaffected pathos, and his wild raving when he imagined that he was ruined and dishonoured. The play may not have been convincing, but the figure of the millionaire who imagined himself a pauper remains graven upon the memory.

But prior to Matthew Ruddock, the embodiment of thrift and niggardly self-denial, Mr. Tree had given us a thriftless, self-indulgent Falstaff, ripe, rich, and luscious to a degree. As a critic said at the time of production at the Haymarket, on January 2nd, 1889—the first performance having been given at the Crystal Palace on September 13th, 1888—perhaps the sensuality of the new Falstaff is gloating rather than roguish, but "if it be so it is not a grievous fault," as "the gloating Falstaff is no doubt the more probable of the two, though not the more Shakespearean;" although it is not altogether easy to imagine a more gloating and less inno-

MR. H. BEERBOHM TREE AS FALSTAFF.

cently roguish libertine than the Falstaff of Shakespeare, judged out of his own mouth. The huge hill of flesh which Mr. Tree contrived by the art of make-up to apparently impose upon his own slender personality was a masterpiece of realism. The huge stomach, the elephantine legs, the bloated, ruddy cheeks, the rolling, bleared, watery eyes, were marvellously assumed; the voice acquired an oily richness and the unctuous hoarseness sequent upon much sack,—the whole impersonation a graceless caricature of a gentleman, as Mr. Tree once called the fat knight. Those who saw him in the part will not easily forget the burly old rascal, with his broad jests and amorous leers, his shameless boasting, unblushing lying, and pitiful pretence of dignity.

It was on the occasion of Mr. Tree's first appearance in this part that a most embarrassing *contretemps* occurred. The actor who is always nervous when essaying a new *rôle*, noticed soon after his appearance that the audience began to smile, then to titter audibly. This naturally encouraged him. "They're taking my Falstaff all right," he thought, and his nervousness wore off. But the tittering increased to such an extent that the player began to suspect his own powers of amusing them so consumedly, and to wonder whether a cat were crossing the stage. Looking about for the cause of offence, he discovered to his horror that his padded trunks had slipped down, revealing to the delighted audience a pair of lean shanks, admirable for Slender, but absurd for the fat knight.

There was nothing for it but to waddle to the wings, be re-trussed, and reappear with as good grace as possible. Naturally, the obvious pun upon Tree's trunks kept the comic journals agog for a week; and afterwards, to retrieve his reputation, as Mr. Tree whimsically says, he was compelled to reappear in the part at the Haymarket, and although it was utterly unsuited to him, managed to win favour in it, and to keep up his trunks.

Naturally, Falstaff was as unlike Gringoire as two types of humanity could be, equally in body and mind; yet Mr. Tree played both characters on the same night for a considerable time,—an "object lesson" in versatility perhaps never excelled even by David Garrick himself, master of lightning-changes as he was.

Upon Triplet in *Masks and Faces*, as played

once by Mr. Tree, there is no need to dwell. It was an excellent performance, true art in its truth to nature, and equally acceptable in its grim pathos and whimsical humour; nor is it necessary to deal at length with his impersonation of King John, to which brief reference is subsequently made, as it is not yet familiar to the public, who will, however, one day recognise in it all the grip of character which has won for Mr. Tree his reputation as one of the most intellectual players of the period.

The rendering of a dual *rôle* in any play must of necessity handicap an actor, yet one of Mr. Tree's most marked successes was made in the characters of Lucien Laroque and Luversan in Mr. Buchanan's adaptation of MM. Jules Mary and Georges Grisier's *Roger la Honte, A Man's Shadow*, produced at the Haymarket Theatre for the first time on September 12th, 1889. A melodramatic, "penny-plain-and-twopence-coloured" sort of piece, although improved by Mr. Buchanan in the process of adaptation, *A Man's Shadow* might well have seemed a doubtful card to play before a Haymarket audience; but by admirable staging, excellent acting all round, and a peculiarly picturesque impersonation by Mr. Tree, it proved a success. And in this dual *rôle* Mr. Tree had an opportunity of practising the art of conveying differences of appearance and character by the slightest touches. Essentially the "shadow" of the amiable, handsome, refined, affectionate, honourable young merchant Lucien Laroque, the scoundrel Luversan was brutal, repulsive, cruel, vulgar, and unprincipled; and yet these very opposite traits were conveyed by such minute details as the substitution of an impudent little scarlet bow for the flowing ends of a highly respectable blue and white spotted necktie, the change of a hat and of the turn of an eyebrow, the addition of a "bang" to the hair, the buttoning of a coat, and the change of voice from a full manly tone to a curious falsetto. In a moment the tender father, the devoted husband, became transformed into the brutal blackmailer, the pitiless villain, the paltry thief. To those who were not familiar with the mystery and potentiality of make-up, the identity of the same actor with Laroque and Luversan would have seemed impossible, and yet, upon critical inspection, the change was found to be the result of a number of very minute differences, marked by a master-hand.

Always indefatigable, always sighing like a modern Alexander for new worlds to conquer, Mr. Tree made another essay at Shakespearean acting by appearing as King John in a revival of that play at the Crystal Palace on September 19th, emphasising the craft and cunning of the coward-king with excellent subtlety and striking effect. The death-scene was a triumph of realistic agony, and the impersonation as interesting as the occasion—a revival of the great play after a hiatus of nearly a quarter of a century.

On April 3rd, 1890, Mr. Tree added one more delightful study to the list of his more benign impersonations. As the Abbé Dubois, in Mr. Sydney Grundy's adaptation of MM. Busnach and Cauvin's *Le Sécret de la Terreuse*, called *The Village Priest*, Mr. Tree once more showed that he was as much at home in the gentler, nobler kind of character, as in the creation of masterly villains. The recipient, under the seal of the confessional, of a terrible secret, there comes a moment in the placid life of the old village priest when he is bewildered by two promptings,—the clerical instinct urging him not to break his vow and so alienate himself from his Church ; the voice of humanity telling him that he must not let the innocent suffer longer for the guilty, and that justice must be done, even though hearts may be broken and innocent lives spoiled. The transition from the gentle, whimsical old man, with no anxiety more onerous than that for his beloved flowers, to the soul-torn priest halting between two opinions, so loth to hurt the innocent representatives of a dead hypocrite, yet so unwilling that injustice should be done to any living soul, was admirable, and one of the crucial moments of the play,—a moment which might easily have failed to convince an audience somewhat sceptical as to modern miracles —was a triumph, thanks to perfect acting.

Gentle and whimsical, tender and manly, old in years but young in heart, a priest but with broad human sympathies, a figure at once touching in its simple dignity and pleasantly picturesque, the Abbé Dubois was a clever and delightful creation, full of fascination, and as lifelike a study as any which Mr. Tree has created.

On October 16th Mr. Tree appeared for the first time as Sir Peter Teazle in a performance of *The School for Scandal* at the Crystal Palace, and despite the number of distinguished actors who have preceded him in the part, he contrived to give his assumption a distinction of its own. Uxorious, doubting, doting, torn by jealousy, yet jealous of his wife's honour even more than his own, the new Sir Peter was not only an interesting but a sympathetic figure, capable of compelling respect, and never forgetting, even in the most bitter moment of his disillusionment, that he was a gentleman, nor the restraint which a remembrance that *noblesse oblige* must always compel.

On Monday, November 3rd, in pursuance of a novel and somewhat courageous policy of breaking the run of successful plays, and devoting, from time to time, Monday evenings for the exploitation of new pieces, Mr. Tree produced an original comedy called *Beau Austin*, by Mr. W. E. Henley and Mr. Robert Louis Stevenson. Mr. Tree was the Beau, admirably made up in the bewigged, quizzing-glassed, short-waisted, rolled-collar-coated, beaver-hatted, tasselled-caned, and tight-pantalooned mode of seventy years ago, and his dress and deportment were interesting studies. The hero of an intrigue worthy of the age of pinchbeck politeness and shoddy sentiment, Mr. Tree made his Beau Austin the veritable incarnation of polished heartlessness and artificiality. In this he was right, but all human interest was so entirely hidden beneath the veneer of manners, that the piece took no hold upon the feelings, the heart did not beat one atom more rapidly, no single tear rose to the eyes, no throb of indignation stirred the pulse throughout the whole representation of a story of girlish credulity, pitiless betrayal, and a final flicker of remorse upon the part of the profligate Beau. In a perfectly charming Prologue Mr. Henley struck the key-note of the comedy thus :—

> "'To all and singular,' as Dryden says,
> We bring a fancy of those Georgian days
> Whose style still breathed a faint and fine perfume
> Of old-world courtliness and old-world bloom ;
> When speech was elegant, and talk was fit,
> For slang had not been canonised as wit ;
> When manners reigned, when breeding had the wall,
> And Women—yes !—were ladies first of all ;
> When Grace was conscious of its gracefulness,
> And man—though Man !—was not ashamed to dress.
> •   •   •   •   •   •

> "A sketch, a shadow, of the brave old time;
> A hint of what it might have held sublime;
> A dream, an idyl, call it what you will,
> Of man, still Man, and woman—Woman still!"

The promise of the Prologue was scarcely fulfilled in the play. Mr. Tree played the Beau as probably no other actor in London could have played it, realising with almost irritating fidelity the contemptible, paltry affectation and puerile vanity of the character, whose smirking and posturing and pompous speeches made it so impossible to give him credit for the possession of any sincerity or heart. The Beau was little more than a sort of sublimated Horatio Sparkins, and in an age when women were "ladies first of all" it seemed incredible that even a silly, sentimental schoolgirl like Dorothy Musgrave could have been consumed by a passion for such a middle-aged bundle of affectations. Mr. Tree made all that he could of the self-satisfied, self-conscious, self-worshipping George Austin; but with all his artistic elaboration of "business" and make-up, his deliberate delivery of polite platitudes, his finicking manipulation of his quizzing-glass, his Regency, gingerbread manners and easy morals, reminding one every moment of that "fourth of the fools and oppressors called George," he only left the impression of a contemptible creature devoid of all true manliness, vain as a woman, lustful as a satyr, petty and paltry as he was posturing—an animated clothes-screen, an advertisement for some Georgian Turveydrop, a poor thing, all leather and prunella. That Beau Austin became such as this in Mr. Tree's hands was excellent proof of the actor's art, but only made any appeal to the hearts of an audience the more futile. As a series of studies of the dress and manners of the period, and of exquisite stage pictures of the old Pantiles, when "trifling Tunbridge" was the chosen resort of the beaux and belles of that trifling age, *Beau Austin* was charming; but the whole thing seemed so superficial, so dependent upon quaint dress and old-world affectations, that it was not altogether easy to think of the vain and silly puppets on the stage as "man, still Man, and woman—Woman still." The climax of the play was curiously characteristic of its pervading sentiment. *Beau Austin* was saturated with snobbishness; and when at last the profligate Beau and the frail Dorothy are recognised publicly as future man and wife, it is only fitting that the dominant consideration in the mind of the Tunbridge Wells Sparkins should be one of horror that the superfine sensibilities of His Royal Highness the Duke of York should have been outraged by a "scene" on the Pantiles in which the brother of the girl whom Sparkins has betrayed slaps the Beau in the face *coram populo*, and under the Royal Nose of the Duke. All the potential pathos and passion go for nothing when it is made so painfully evident that a tender regard for the feelings of the puffy "Royal Highness" was reckoned of infinitely higher importance than the honour of a woman or the good faith of a man. A remarkably able study so far as Mr. Tree is concerned, Beau Austin will always be interesting as a stage reincarnation of a type which can well be spared in real life, a revival of the unfittest in human nature—a man without manliness, a *petit-maître*, an apotheosised tailor's dummy, an anything you please save a man or a gentleman in the only worthy sense of the words, a clever portrait of an unworthy subject, the central figure in a series of charming pictures of English society under the *régime* of that so-called " First Gentleman of Europe " and caricature of kings, George the Fourth.

Mr. Tree revived *Called Back* on November 10th, resuming his original *rôle* of Paolo Macari with complete success, and in pursuance of his " Monday Night " policy also gave a representation of *The Red Lamp* on December 8th, *Captain Swift* on December 15th, and subsequently other favourite pieces in his *répertoire*, resuming his original *rôles* with obvious zest, and making the characters riper and even more interesting than before.

On January 15th, 1891, Mr. Tree produced *The Dancing Girl*, a strong, daring drama by Mr. Henry Arthur Jones, with immediate and unqualified success. His own assumption of the part of a spendthrift, ruined Duke of Guisebury, who has gone to the dogs, but yet is full of excellent instincts, was as subtle as ever ; and in the great scene, "The Last Feast," before he puts poison to his lips, he was powerful and effective to a degree. His "business" was, as usual, fertile in significance ; and the whole impersonation interesting, as Mr. Tree, of all living actors, could make so well-conceived a character. The play was not without inconsistencies both of incident and character-detail, but Mr. Tree's creation of the principal *rôle* was entirely consistent. From end to end of the drama he was obviously a man of good instincts, spoiled by conditions which, acting upon a nature essentially weak, made him morally and socially the sport of circumstances, the creature of momentary impulse, a living example of the struggle between the noble and ignoble instincts of human nature—the latter proving their power, and the former, and weaker, going to the wall.

Vice and virtue, youth and age, stalwart manhood and slinking currishness, every species of human nature under all conceivable conditions, these are the types with which Mr. Tree has already enriched the stage. And he has still youth on his side. He is on almost the topmost rung of the dramatic ladder. To-day, young as he is, and few years as he has been upon the stage, he has already earned for himself a place of honour upon the roll which bears in brilliant blazonry the names of the foremost actors of the century. Who shall say what new triumphs are in store for him?

What would it matter to me if I owned all the money in the country so long as I couldn't turn out a piece of work like that—

Cyrus Blenkarn.
; The Middleman.

E. S. WILLARD.

THERE was a time when it seemed to the habitual playgoer that the dramatic doom of Mr. E. S. Willard was to perpetually "smile and smile and be a villain." And, of a truth, there were reasons enough for such an imagining. A suavity of manner, coupled with a sardonic sneer of bitterest import, dark, expressive eyes, clear-cut features, a good carriage, and a set of gleaming teeth worth a whole box of make-up to an impersonator of gentlemanly scoundrelism, seemed to have marked Mr. Willard as the society villain *par excellence* of modern melodrama; and that very amiable and excellent gentleman appeared to be fated to endure a dual existence—an upright, kindly, altogether admirable Jekyll by day—a Hyde, without the physical horror, by night.

But, brilliant as Mr. Willard's villains were; keen as was the delight which they afforded to sensitive and romantic souls to whom intermittent blood-curdling is a necessity of existence, Fate, juster and kinder than she is commonly reputed, had better things in store for a man of such excellent gifts, and in Captain Herbert Skinner, the Spider of to-day—the swell mobsman who cracked cribs in evening dress, and whose only regret for robbing his host's sideboard was that he would miss the plate when next he dined with him—was hidden the Claudius, King of Denmark, of to-morrow.

Like most actors who have made their way to the front of their profession, Mr. Willard graduated in the provinces. His first appearance was made upon the stage of the Theatre Royal, Weymouth, on Boxing Day, 1869, in the unimportant *rôle* of Second Officer in *The Lady of Lyons*, and it was only after a good many years of very varied work in the country that he came to London, to win name and fame and honour by hard work, an obvious earnestness, and a dramatic gift far above the average.

It is interesting, in the light of his subsequent success, to recall some of his experiences in those early days, when he "went the western circuit," migrated to Glasgow as "responsible utility," where Mr. Sothern, of Lord Dundreary fame, engaged him for a tour, during which he appeared as Captain de Boots in *Dundreary Married and Settled*, Mr. Smith in *David Garrick*, and Asa Trenchard in *Our American Cousin*. Then came seasons at Plymouth, Scarborough, Belfast, Dublin, where he played John Ferne in *Progress*, and first attracted some attention; Birkenhead, Newcastle, Scarborough, Sunderland; a second season in Newcastle, where he appeared as Romeo, Macduff, and Iago; and Bradford, where he again made some mark as Edmund in *King Lear*.

Ten years ago the name of Mr. E. S. Willard was virtually unknown to the great playgoing public of the metropolis. Now, after spending sixteen of his thirty-seven years of life on the stage, there are few names more familiar or more popular, and this honourable position in the dramatic world has been won by much hard and estimable work.

Mr. Willard's first appearance on the London stage was also on a Boxing Day, in 1875, when he undertook the part of Alfred Highflyer in *A Roland for an Oliver*, at Covent Garden; and he appeared at the same time as Antonio in *The Merchant of Venice*, both pieces preceding the pantomime. Then came more long provincial tours, and an endless variety of impersonations, including Edgar in *King Lear*, Eugene Aram, Orlando Middlemark in *A Lesson in Love*, Sidney Daryl in *Society*, Horace Holmcroft in *The New Magdalen*, Robert Folliott in *The Shaughraun*, Hector Placide in *Led Astray;* Dubosc and Lesurques in *The Lyons Mail*, Macbeth, Claude Melnotte, Lord Clancarty, Sir Peter Teazle, Sir Harcourt Courtley, and Richard Arkwright, Mr. Willard supporting Miss Helen Barry as her leading man; and later on appearing as Benedick, Charles Surface, Young Marlow, Frank Annesley, Ham Peggotty, Charles Middlewick, Augustus Vere in *Married in Haste*, Lionel Leveret in *Old Soldiers*, Jack

Dudley in *Ruth's Romance*, Fletcher in H. J Byron's *Uncle*, and in one of Mr. H. A. Jones's earliest pieces, called *Elopement*, until his final and decisive return to London in 1881.

In that year he appeared at the Imperial Theatre as Sir Harcourt Courtley, De Lesparre in *Led Astray*, and Peter Hayes in *Arkwright's Wife*, playing in the afternoon at the Aquarium and in the evening in Brighton ; and subsequently he appeared at the Alexandra Palace as Frank Hawthorn in *Extremes*, Cyril in *Cyril's Success*, Sir Thomas Clifford in *The Hunchback*, and as Charles Surface.

Intense devotion to his art, an excellent habit of thinking for himself, and so importing originality even into the most familiar parts, indomitable courage and perseverance, have been the secrets of Mr. Willard's success. Nor is his dramatic method less admirable. Vigour, restrained always from lapsing into violence ; refinement of manner, speech, and style—never to be mistaken for affectation ; subtle and highly-finished art, which extracts the utmost value from every word and gesture ; a tenderness on occasion ; a passionate self-abandonment in moments demanding moral heroism; a stern intensity in depicting indignation or sorrow; a sincerity and refinement free from cloying sentimentality or smug self-satisfaction in love scenes, have proved his versatility, his good taste, his control over the resources of his art.

Like all actors of somewhat striking physique, he possesses *les qualités de ses défauts*. He rarely quite obliterates himself in his part; but as Mr. E. S. Willard has the good fortune to enjoy a well-deserved popularity, it is, at all events in the eyes of very many *habitués* of the theatre, no serious fault that his personal identity is disguised rather than lost in the characters which he assumes.

When the curtain has fallen and Mr. Willard has returned to his pretty home in Blenheim Road, St. John's Wood, the realistic professor of villainy in all its branches becomes an amiable, refined, somewhat studious gentleman, of decidedly æsthetic proclivities, with a passion for Swinburne's melodious poetry, quaint old furniture of blackest oak, dainty old china, and all the artistic *entourage* of a man of taste.

Out of doors a well-kept lawn and garden,

rich in flowers, and a conservatory, in which the actor cultivates successfully the Japanese chrysanthemums and colourful carnations in which his soul delights, speak well for his devotion to nature; while, within, a host of professional souvenirs, such as Tarquin's leopard-skin, Dick Dugdale's revolver, the Spider's stick, and Captain Ezra Promise's spurs and " Book of Hours," speak well for his devotion to his art. Portraits of a host of dramatic and literary celebrities, original editions of Swinburne, Dickens, Tennyson, Browning, and other of his favourite authors, and some twenty editions of Shakespeare, divide the honours with old blue china, Persian rugs and curios, and the thousand and one odds and ends which lend so indefinable but real a charm to the home of a man who is an artist in soul as well as by courtesy.

Mr. Willard is essentially a lover of home-life, and has a holy horror of notoriety. The cheap delight of being the centre of a circle of admiring and effusive enthusiasts in the gilded cages of the Mrs. Leo Hunters of to-day has no attraction for him; he does not "pine for higher society" than that of his fellow-artists and beautiful and gentle wife, and in all that he does he is both on and off the stage the same earnest, sincere, honourable, self-respecting, and kindly-natured man. He has made many friends, and his successful career is followed by them with a keen interest which could only result from a feeling of personal liking and esteem.

Mr. Willard's amiable disposition and high personal character have won him many friends, and his charming wife dispenses the most delightful hospitality, to which an added charm is given by the cordial geniality of her popular actor-husband.

It is perhaps a little curious that a player of so much power should in his private life enjoy environment by things purely, almost femininely, æsthetic in their tone, but the combination of the dual nature thus displayed is no doubt one of the secrets of Mr. Willard's histrionic success, as it evidences an adaptability of mind and disposition as valuable on the stage as it is interesting off it, and emphasises the truth of Mr. Willard's theory of the necessity of versatility in his art: " An actor must act, and not trust to an author fitting him with a character suitable to his particular mannerisms;" and how fully he has realised this idea in his own person may be gathered from the *dictum* of the trade journal of the pottery business, which said of his Cyrus Blenkarn, in *The Middleman*, that "one would imagine, from its correctness to character and the furnace work, that some excitable and clever potter had become an actor, not that an actor had, for this piece only, become a potter."

So tender a conscience has Mr. Willard upon the question of fidelity in his representations and stage "business," that he studied the garb, mien, and deportment of half the Nonconformist ministers in London before appearing as the Rev. Judah Llewellyn in Mr. Jones's play; and in Mr. Berlyn's poetical version of François Coppée's delightful piece *Le Luthier de Cremone* the "bowing" of Filippo's violin is the result of study, although the actual music is made by a player posted out of sight of the audience, just beneath the open window by the side of which the hump-backed, gifted violin-maker bends over the instrument which he has made with so much loving labour.

When *The Lights o' London* was produced with such remarkable success at the Princess's Theatre on September 10th, 1881, Mr. Willard got his first great chance of making a name upon the metropolitan stage, after years of varied and useful experience in the provinces. He seized it with avidity, and his Clifford Armytage was only second to the hero of Mr. Sims's clever drama in interest and individuality,—a thankless part to play, that of a cold-blooded, currish, traitorous scoundrel, a nineteenth-century Jacob who had improved upon the cunning of his biblical prototype by the aid of all the resources of civilisation. But, like a true artist, Mr. Willard accepted the hisses of the honest critics in the pit and gallery as what they were—the sincerest tribute which they could pay to the excellent art with which he played the villain.

Jealous of the manly qualities of Harold, grudging him alike the love of the woman upon whom he himself had cast amorous eyes, and the just inheritance of his father's wealth, the supple, insinuating rascal set his snares and planned a dual downfall for the hero. His success was absolute, and Mr. Willard's quiet method of conveying the triumph of mind over matter, of callous, cruel, unscrupulous selfishness and hate over manly, unsuspecting honesty and goodwill, was faultless.

And all through the play the same careful and complete contrast was sustained. In make-up, in the unctuous voice, thickening on occasion into the hoarseness of passion or sliding into the sibilation of malignancy, in dress, in movement, gesture, in every microscopical detail by means of which the workings of an evil mind could be translated into visible form or audible sound, Clifford Armytage was the moral and physical antithesis of his hero-cousin, adding thus to the value of both parts, and intensifying, as only the introduction of artistic light and shade can, the interest of the whole work.

With this creation Mr. Willard planted his foot firmly upon the ladder of dramatic fame, and from that day to this he has quietly, resolutely, and almost without exception, mounted higher with each new impersonation.

Crammed with exciting incidents and remarkable characters, and labouring beneath the burden of a too-complicated plot, *The Romany Rye*, produced by Mr. Wilson Barrett at the Princess's Theatre on June 10th, 1882, enabled Mr. Willard to create one more stage villain in the person of Philip Royston, the young Squire of Craigsnest, who won, by very virtue of his consummate vice, the unstinted approval of the public.

Cowardly and cruel to the ultimate degree, Philip Royston, who plots the ruin of his elder brother, Jack Hearne, consorts with scoundrels dipped deep in the regulation melodramatic dye of darkest hue, and acts the part of a pitiless betrayer to a trusting girl, was invested by Mr. Willard with so much charm, and surrounded by so fascinating an atmosphere of romance, that for once the audience, whose appreciation of such characters is usually manifested by groans and hisses, metaphorically took the romantic rascal to their hearts, and lifted him from the villainous to the heroic.

The triumph of the actor was complete. A more insinuating, gentlemanly scoundrel than Philip Royston could not have been created. At times, too, Mr. Willard exhibited a callous cruelty which told with excellent effect; and from first to last, throughout all the *sturm und drang* of a melodrama so rich in exciting incidents as to run the risk of surfeiting the audience with sensationalism, Philip Royston remained a noticeable figure, refreshingly cool in its imperturbable, consistent rascality, and as uncompromisingly villainous as even the most *blasé* connoisseur of stage criminals could demand.

Honours were divided between the audacity of the authors and the art of the actor in the case of Mr. Willard's quite remarkable creation of Captain Herbert Skinner, *alias* the Spider, in *The Silver King*. This dandy burglar, who divided his time between dining with duchesses and robbing them of their jewels; who was equally at home in a boudoir in Mayfair or a "boozing-ken" in Ratcliffe Highway; whose debonair criminality was combined with a patrician ease of bearing which induced the best people to accept him at his own valuation,—was a new thing on the stage, and as all the world is secretly, if not admittedly, perpetually panting for novelty as the very salt of life, the Spider was the hit of the season.

True, nobody in front of the foot-lights believed in him. He was obviously, obtrusively impossible. But the authors believed in him, and the actor believed in him—as a striking stage figure, and they were right. The art of the actor enabled him to compel the audience to discredit their senses, to stultify their judgment, to accept and to applaud the impossible. It was as though the Spider had recognised the onus laid upon him, and had said to himself: "They don't believe in me. Very well—they shall!" and then presented himself to them as a personality—peculiar perhaps, but there in the flesh, substantial, palpable, not to be argued or reasoned out of existence.

So marked an individuality had this character, that Mr. Willard was known as the Spider outside the theatre; and one night, riding in an omnibus, the actor was much amused by the collapse of an abortive attempt to give him short change being clinched by the driver's dry comment to the conductor, as the fare got down and entered the theatre: "No good trying it on '*im*, Bill! Don't you know who he is? *He's the 'Spider'!*"

The veneer of a fine-gentleman air, with its under-surface of brutality and its rough excrescences of irrepressible vulgarity breaking through here and there, were most admirably assumed. The Spider was just as delicate a caricature in his assumption of gentlemanly airs as he was in his autocratic ordering about of his vulgar accomplices in crime; the meretricious varnish of an affectation of aristocratic polish only served to throw into coarser relief the innate vulgarity of the man; and Mr. Willard threw himself

MR. WILLARD AS THE SPIDER.

into his part with so much artistic zeal that, instead of the gentleman-burglar seeming an absurd anomaly, fit only for the pages of a "penny dreadful" and the horrifying of sensation-seekers in the servants' hall, it became an interesting study and a new stage type, a triumph of art over artificiality, a metamorphosis of a daring, impossible conception into a creation which, if not convincing, was consistent, unique, and effective to a rare degree.

Mr. Willard's make-up in this part was so striking, and his gleaming teeth played so important a part in helping the illusion, that an *habitué* of the theatre was much amused one night by being accosted in the *foyer* of the theatre by a rather seedy stranger, who, after sundry apologies, announced that he had got a recipe for a wonderful tooth-powder, and innocently inquired if the critic thought that there was "any chance of getting Mr. Willard to be photographed as an advertisement of the elixir!"

As the Holy Clement, in *Claudian*, Mr. Willard enjoyed the privilege of launching with admirable elocutionary effect, and a bitterness of denunciation only conceivable in a truly pious character, the most blighting, baneful, withering, and altogether awful curse ever heard upon the stage. Stabbed by the impious and licentious Claudian, he staggered across the stage, and, supporting himself against a rock, hurled gaspingly, with many moribund but muscular spasms, a curse unrivalled out of the pages of Barham.

But, maugre this terrible curse, which, be it said, was delivered with excellent art, the hollow tones and broken sequence caused by impending death being admirably assumed, the Holy Clement was so interesting a figure, so artistically conceived and embodied, that it was lamentable that the exigencies of the plot snatched him from the audience so early in the play.

Enough scope, however, was given in the part to enable the actor to give convincing evidence of the versatility which is indispensable in the manufacture of an artist of the first quality. From the impudent devilry of the Spider to the venerable sanctity of the Holy Clement was a change as utter as it was successful, and Mr. Willard proved by it to demonstration that he was essentially an actor, not a mere projector of so many variations of his own personality.

As a fit and consistent companion picture to Mr. Wilson Barrett's boyish Prince of Denmark, the Princess's revival of *Hamlet* was remarkable for a comparatively youthful and refreshingly unconventional Claudius. Mr. Willard's King was, in its way and its degree, as fine, as original, as striking an assumption as Mr. Barrett's Hamlet. In both, intelligibility and a "sweet reasonableness" of conception were boldly opposed to the constrictive convention and traditional obscurity of the character.

Mr. Willard's Claudius was a full-blooded, sensual, animal King, instinct with the spirit of a court all lies and lust; a muscular, eupeptic, pleasure-loving creature, caring for nothing beyond the indulgence of his appetites; audacious in his selfishness; cruel, cynical, contemptuous of the loyal, loving student-soul which he could not even understand.

With such a Claudius the whole play became

at once more lucidly intelligible, and so robust a King was the legitimate and necessary complement to a boyish Hamlet and a Gertrude whose charms were yet lacking some years of their decadence. The unholy loves of Claudius and the Queen were comprehensible in this fresh light, and the new reading of the part was not only necessary to the consistency of the scheme of the whole production, but absolutely and convincingly natural.

The careless consciousness of power, the fierce animal passion leading to crime, the subsequent soul-sickening fear, were indicated by Mr. Willard with splendid lucidity and force; his elocution was a delight to those who love to hear the sublimities of Shakespeare worthily voiced; and the impersonation taken as a whole was completely artistic, picturesque, powerful, and harmonious.

It is given to few moderns to assume the classic garb of ancient Rome with picturesque effect, and in the great play of *Junius*, produced at the Princess's Theatre on February 26th, 1885, it was not the fault of Sextus Tarquin and his boon companions that their entrance was provocative of a smile, as they lounged into the banqueting-hall of Tarquin's palace, flower-wreathed in strictly classical but lamentably unbecoming fashion. Rose-wreathed revellers are romantic enough on canvas, but it is difficult to imagine the reality as not having been just an atom absurd. But whatever tendency to an irreverent smile might have been provoked by the artificial roses, soon gave place in the case of Sextus Tarquin to unlimited admiration of the actor's art.

It was quickly apparent that Mr. Willard had in store for his audience a bold and brilliant character-study of a splendid sinner, a clue to whose nature was given in a fine passage, in which he rebuts the dictum of his more effeminate brother that good wine should be quaffed with slowness and discretion. With exuberant animal delight in sensual pleasures Sextus retorts:—

> "Oh, thou sluggard! Joy
> Is in the rapid seizure of the joy!
> Methinks that Jove, the fashioner of kings
> Gave his own lightning to my fiery blood!
> War is with me no long-drawn tedious craft,
> But the swift bliss of foeman grappling foe;

> Love is with me no shepherd's timorous tale
> Piped on his reed, and wasting hours in sighs;
> But a fierce gladness, like a mountain stream,
> Flashing back sunlight as it storms along."

The symbols used by Sextus may sound a little conventional to-day, but they are unquestionably just what he would have used in an age when Nature was still the great inspirer, and culture as yet only in its embryonic stage of affectation. And it conveys the dominant characteristics of the tyrant with admirable conciseness. Mr. Willard declaimed the passage magnificently, and his whole bearing throughout the revel was superbly daring and defiant. When, flushed with wine, the revellers boasted of the virtues of their wives, and Tarquin made a wager with the married Romans as to the occupations of the women during their absence, a quest was made, and when it was over, Sextus told Casca what he had found in the house of Collatinus, the husband of Lucretia, in a brief but very significant passage:—

> "Amidst the maidens at the loom,
> By the chaste Household Gods, there sat a form
> So fair, so young, so beautifully calm,
> Unconsciously we hushed our tread, and stood
> Gazing and awed, as in some holy temple."

To this Casca, wondering at the tyrant's words, replied :

> "Why, Sextus, thou speak'st worthily; thou mov'st
> My rugged soldier's breast. I honour thee
> For honouring Virtue thus."

And then, with a splendid outburst of contempt, the brutal, mocking animality of the libertine bursts forth :

> "For honouring Virtue?
> What prat'st thou of, dull man? I spoke of Beauty,
> And I thought of Love!"

Presently came the crime of Tarquin, treated with perfect tact. The temptation, the crime, the remorse, all were conveyed with consummate skill, and the crushing of the egoistic, sensual tyrant, hitherto fearing neither the gods nor man, was portrayed with fine effect in Mr. Willard's masterly delivery of an eloquent passage :

> "What noise is that? Who stirs? O Gods! I start
> At my own footfall, quake at my own shadow.
> So this is fear! this sinking of the heart,
> This freezing horror in the veins, this awe
> In solitude; yet this recoil from man!
>   *   *   *   *   *
> Fell goddess Fear! I who till now defied thee,
> Feel thy pale power, and bow with trembling limbs."

From this terrible moment Nemesis stalked towards the wretched sensualist with unfaltering feet, leading to the startling climax in the final act.

The palace of Tarquin was a magnificent realisation of imperial pomp and luxury. Tarquin, utterly demoralised and in abject fear, tried to forget in the splendour of his surroundings the craven dread of coming doom which was eating away his heart. He sat upon a golden throne, the marble steps of which were strewn with the skins of tigers; his household guards surrounded him in all the panoply of armour; courtiers still fawned, and, to the eye at least, his pride and power and luxury were still unshaken. But gloom sat upon the brow of the Greek philosopher of the court, and Tarquin, the destroyer of life and honour, knew that his hour had come.

A noise was heard in the distance, and a procession approached, to the cry of "Room for the Household Gods!" Collatinus, Valerius, Junius, and a host of citizens and soldiers brought the dead Lucretia to the very feet of the libertine; Junius told the people of the crime ; the tyrant, at bay, made one mad dash for life and liberty, but failed, and was dragged to the foot of the throne, forced to his knees, and stabbed to the heart by Junius, with the wild cry :

> "Kneel, Tarquin, kneel!
> Lucretia, tell the Gods that Rome is free!"

With this splendid tableau the play ended, and it was unanimously shown by the audience that in their judgment the Tarquin of Mr. Willard was a bold, powerful study, and a worthy pendant to the Claudius which in *Hamlet* marked him as an actor of equal power and originality.

In *Hoodman Blind*, produced with great success at the Princess's on August 18th, 1885, Mr. Willard was entrusted with the work of creating a villain of a type new to him. The dainty cigarette, punctiliously pointed moustache, and faultless *tenue* of the "Spider," and the picturesque profligacy of Sextus Tarquin, gave place to the grizzled, middle-aged, hard-featured, plainly-dressed figure of a rascally land-agent, by whose wiles and roguery the handsome young Buckinghamshire farmer was to be made miserable and penniless.

And as Mark Lezzard, Mr. Willard again displayed a masterly conception of character, an instinct for making-up with perfect effect and without exaggeration, and a grim power of portraying commonplace villainy, which once more justified the high opinion of his critics.

Consumed by a hopeless passion for the heroine, a passion fierce and more engrossing even than his love of money, Mark Lezzard was a well-thought-out and vigorously rendered study of hard, unscrupulous middle-age, labouring under a passion so misplaced, so hopeless, but so

MR. E. S. WILLARD AS MARK LEZZARD.

deeply rooted, that it only served to intensify all the evil qualities of his nature, and became transformed, in the fierce crucible of despair, into malignant hate. With quiet power, holding himself admirably free from rant and raving, Mr. Willard made Mark Lezzard an almost tragic figure. Condemned still to play the villain, he appeared to revel in creating a new species of the genus; and, as Paganini drew marvellously varied melody from a single string, so the actor, vowed to dramatic villainy, proved his talent by drawing from each new *rôle* some marked variations from its predecessors.

As Glaucias, in the brilliant production of *Clito*, on May 1st, 1886, Mr. Willard was allotted some of the wittiest and bitterest epigrams, and delivered them to perfection. The veritable living embodiment of the voluptuous, cruel luxury of pagan Greece, Glaucias is as cynical as he is selfish, as satirical as he is pitiless in the pursuit of his own evil will. The audacious imperturbability of the libertine, the insolence of vice of which he is the incarnation, were rendered with the utmost effect

MR. E. S. WILLARD AS CAPTAIN EZRA PROMISE.

by the actor; and the merciless, poisoned wit with which he expressed his contempt for Clito and the band of patriots with whom he was allied, flew from his sharp tongue with a spontaneity which added much to its effect.

The callous animality, the caustic irony, the cynical contemptuousness, the calculating cruelty of the Greek voluptuary, were exhibited with intense force, while the more delicate lights and shadows of the character were indicated with a subtlety and finesse which made the creation very realistic and convincing. Indeed, a more perfect foil to the classic grace and simple dignity of Clito could not have been conceived, and Glaucias proved a notable addition to Mr. Willard's growing gallery of stage villains.

Although the romantic drama of the Cavalier and Roundhead era, *The Lord Harry*, enjoyed but a brief spell of dramatic life, it sufficed to afford Mr. Willard an opportunity of creating a scoundrel of a new type. As Captain Ezra Promise, a Roundhead rascal whose lips were devoted in about equal measure to lies and biblical phrases, and whose rigid Puritanism but served as a cloak for a raging passion of unholy desire, Mr. Willard was superb. The sham asceticism of the canting rogue, his treachery and malignity, his not wholly assumed severity and religious zeal, his bitter envy, hatred, and malice towards the ruffling, handsome Cavalier whom he professed to despise, were all excellently rendered. No gesture, no movement of limb or feature, no harsh inflection of tone which could accentuate the character, was omitted. The impersonation was exceptionally artistic and curiously picturesque. Grim and often despicable as Ezra Promise was often made, the actor's delicate art contrived to import into the assumption now and then an element of pathos, and thus compelled the occasional pity which usually exists, at least potentially, when an impersonation is an unqualified success.

Upon the closing of the Princess's season in 1886 Mr. Willard migrated to the Haymarket Theatre, appearing in a revival of *Jim the Penman*, playing the part of James Ralston, the gentlemanly forger, with characteristic finish and quiet force.

While playing at the Princess's as a member

of Mr. Barrett's company, Mr. Willard appeared at various *matinées* with great success, making an excellent impression in Robertsonian comedy in 1882, at the Crystal Palace, appearing as Dunscombe Dunscombe in *M.P.*, as Lord Ptarmigant in *Society;* and as Master Walter in *The Hunchback*. At the Gaiety he made an excellent King William in *Lady Clancarty;* and at various other *matinées* he appeared as Dr. Vasseur, in *Won by Honours;* as Tom Pinch; Rawdon Scudamore in *Hunted Down*, Wildrake in *The Love Chase*, and Iachimo in *Cymbeline*.

In 1887 and 1888 Mr. Willard appeared in many characters and upon various stages, his impersonations during that period embracing Tony Saxon, in Mr. Henry Arthur Jones's drama *Hard Hit*, produced at the Haymarket on January 17th, 1887, which give him a chance of incisive, quietly effective acting in the part of a ruined country gentleman who takes his ill-luck with philosophical equanimity; Geoffrey Delamayn, in a Haymarket revival of Wilkie Collins's gloomy but powerful play *Man and Wife*, on March 29th, in which he made the athlete even more brutally cruel than usual, and scored an artistic success; Coranto, in Mr. A. C. Calmour's *Amber Heart*, produced at a Lyceum *matinée* on June 7th, when Mr. Willard delivered his poetical lines with great charm, and revealed a new phase of his talent by appearing as a tender-hearted, loyal and sympathetic man, and a wise and gentle physician; an excellent Captain Hawkesley, in *Still Waters run Deep*, at a Criterion *matinée;* Gonzales, in Ross Neil's romantic play *Loyal Love*, at a Gaiety *matinée* on August 18th, in which part he glossed over an impossibly extreme villain by the excellence of his acting; Richard Dugdale, in *The Pointsman*, by Messrs. R. C. Carton and Cecil Raleigh, produced at the Olympic Theatre on August 29th, which enabled him to depict utter heartless, deliberate villainy with the concentrated power of which he is so complete a master; and Colonel Prescott, in *Held by the Enemy*, at the Olympic, on December 24th, in which he proved capable and incisive as ever.

The thoroughly artistic versatility of Mr. Willard was shown convincingly enough in his impersonation of the Tiger, in the Olympic revival of Tom Taylor's evergreen *Ticket-of-Leave-Man*, on January 28th, 1888. Whether as the frankly brutal villain, with a heart hard as the nether millstone, and a sublime audacity and recklessness, or disguised as the silvery-haired, silver-toned merchant, mild as milk and innocent as an unborn babe, Mr. Willard was faultless. Make-up, bearing, voice, gesture, all were utterly transformed, and testified to the actor's consummate mastery of his art.

In the revival of Tom Taylor and John Saunders' effective drama, *Arkwright's Wife*, on the occasion of Miss Helen Barry's *matinée* at the Prince of Wales's Theatre, on Valentine's Day, 1888, Mr. Willard, as Peter Hayes, scored another notable success. The subtlety with which he conveyed the feeling of the absorption of Peter Hayes in his one idea was thoroughly artistic, and the *rôle* proved to be a quite remarkable assumption, in which Mr. Willard's acting gripped the audience from first to last, and won from them a cordial recognition.

On March 8th, 1888, the arch-villain of the contemporary stage was given an opportunity of distinguishing himself once more in a *rôle* after his histrionic heart. The romantic drama *Christina*, originally produced at the Prince of Wales's Theatre on April 22nd, 1887, was revived at the Olympic. The authors, Messrs. Percy Lynwood and Mark Ambient, had strengthened their original work, and the villain of the piece, Count Freund, could not have been entrusted to better hands than those of Mr. Willard. The actor apparently revelled in the depths of meanness, cowardice, and selfishness in which for the time being he had to sink his moral nature, and he abandoned himself to the ungracious task with heroic self-abnegation. The result was a remarkable creation, a notable if ephemeral stage figure, one more Willardesque, Iago-like villain of the deepest dye.

At a *matinée* at the Prince of Wales's Theatre on March 20th, Mr. Willard enacted the *rôle* of Master Walter in *The Hunchback* with signal success. Always a faultless elocutionist, Mr. Willard did the fullest justice to the text; his make-up was artistic and kept within discreet bounds, and his every word and gesture instinct with significance. The impersonation was a notable one, and helped to confirm the high estimate of Mr. Willard's talent which was now becoming universal.

Upon May 3rd, 1888, in a revival of the tragedy at the Olympic, with Mrs. Bandmann Palmer as Lady Macbeth, Mr. Willard essayed the very difficult *rôle* of Macbeth. Versatile as he had proved himself to be, and entirely admirable as had been his Claudius in the Princess's revival of *Hamlet*, his Macbeth was not so striking an assumption as might have been anticipated. There were excellent moments in it,—moments that were almost great, —but upon the whole there was a lack of conspicuous originality of treatment, and the impersonation, although thoughtful, conscientious, and occasionally striking, was not as distinctly individual as an actor of so much talent might have been expected to make it. It was good, but it was not great, and Mr. Willard's past had led his critics to expect great things of him, whether in Shakespeare or in modern drama, and his Macbeth could only be written down a negative success, inasmuch as it was not a failure.

At an Olympic *matinée* on March 23rd, 1888, and subsequently when the piece went into the evening bill at the same theatre on May 16th, Mr. Willard gave the public a taste of his quality as a picturesque villain and passionate lover in the *rôle* of Count Danella, in the drama *To the Death*, a dramatic version of the very romantic, sensational, and interesting story, "Mr. Barnes of New York."

The terrible vendetta which is the central *motif* of the drama provided the audience with a sequence of sensations, and in the vengeful, subtle Count Danella, with all the fierce passion of the South burning in his veins, yet with ever a cool head and callous heart for intrigue and revenge, Mr. Willard created a remarkably effective stage figure. In the great scene with Marita his passionate outburst of love, despair, and crushing disappointment was an excellent and convincing piece of acting, and marked one more step on the road to the front rank in his art. The *rôle* of Count Danella was not only an effective one in itself, but excellently well suited to Mr. Willard's vivid and picturesque method, nor did he fail to make the most of it.

Never unduly obtrusive, he was always the most interesting figure on the stage, and his creation of the part of the passionate Southerner was a marked artistic success.

When Mr. John Lart rented the Globe Theatre for a revival of his sombre but powerful drama, *The Monk's Room*, Mr. Willard appeared, on October 12th, 1888, in the *rôle* of Sir Darrell Erne, with a success which was anticipated by those who had watched his previous impersonations critically. That Sir Darrell Erne would become in Mr. Willard's hands a thoughtful, earnest study was a foregone conclusion, and it was not surprising to find all the morbid melancholy of the part painted with rare fidelity. But beyond this phase of the character, so easily within Mr. Willard's range, his graceful, tender love-scenes with Eleanor Brandon lent a charm not only to the part, but to the play, infusing into it an element of pure romance and delicate sentiment of enormous value to the drama as a whole. The piece was well received, and Mr. Willard was unanimously acknowledged to have added a fascinating figure to his *répertoire*, and to have given one more proof of his right to rank amongst the leading actors of the day.

After this came a migration to the Shaftesbury Theatre, when Mr. Willard reappeared with success as James Ralston in a revival of *Jim the Penman*, on June 8th, 1889; and also as Captain Howard Leslie, in *My Aunt's Advice*, given on the occasion of Mrs. Kitty Stephens's farewell to the stage on July 9th, after fifty years of acting. But these were only the preliminaries of one more notable and convincing impersonation.

On August 27th, 1889, Mr. Willard achieved one of his greatest successes, and enriched the stage with a really remarkable creation, in the character of Cyrus Blenkarn, in Mr. Henry Arthur Jones's excellent play *The Middleman*.

With public feeling in regard to the relations of capital and labour, of brains and bank balances, excited to a pitch of enthusiasm which would almost deem it an unpardonable sin for a man to possess five pounds of his own and a determination to tyrannically insist on paying them to some other man in payment for work done, the popular success of a drama in which the capitalist is represented as a crafty scoundrel, ready to drive a hard bargain with brains because their possessor is starving, was assured. The spirit of justice to labour, of hand or head, was in the air, and rightly. Nor, be it added, was any jot of sympathy due to the capitalist, the "Middleman" between the inventor and the public, the producer and the consumer, in Mr. Jones's drama. Moreover, the play itself was well written, full of excellent situations and effective contrasts, yet its success was certainly none the less that in some of its most telling passages, some of its most touching incidents, were voiced and painted sentiments and pictures in harmony with the exaggerated feeling of the day.

In *The Middleman* Mr. Willard assumed the *rôle* of an old inventor—a simple, pathetic figure, half blind with ceaseless labour at the potter's wheel and furnace; aged before his time by devotion to his idea of reviving a lost art in glazing pottery; utterly absorbed in his life-work, to the neglect of his interests and even of his well-loved daughter. His whole nature steeped in dogged resolution to succeed or die at his work, there was always a simple dignity about Cyrus Blenkarn—the innate and ineradicable dignity of a man in fierce earnest to realise a worthy aspiration ; and the inventor, poor, purblind, poring, shabby, starving fanatic that he seems, yet compels respect once and for all time.

Engrossed by one idea, alternately rapt to the seventh heaven of enthusiasm by a glimmering promise of success, and cast into an abysmal despair by yet one more failure, the old potter is an intensely pathetic study, elaborated with loving care by author and by actor. But beneath the surface, dormant but never for an instant dead, burns a passionate love for his motherless girl. The inventor is dominant for the most part, but now and again the imperious voice of nature makes itself heard, and the father—loving, tender, anxious, full of self-reproach and tender solicitude—touches all hearts.

But the central idea is not domestic, it is social. It is the *métier* of Cyrus Blenkarn not only to revive, to some degree, all the romance and tragedy of a historical incident familiar to students of the industries of England, but in a greater degree still to body forth the popular ideal of the brainworker of to-day, robbed, tyrannised over, cheated, crushed, by the middleman and his money.

And Mr. Willard has rarely done anything finer than the splendid old enthusiast, slaving, fireless, foodless, desperate, yet buoyed up through all with a prophetic instinct of ultimate triumph. And when that triumph comes; when, after failure has succeeded failure, and no money and no credit for the monomaniac remain; when the last chair in the wretched home has been broken up to feed the insatiable maw of the furnace—when, with an inarticulate, gasping cry, culminating in a hoarse shout of triumph, the middleman, tempting still with his offers to purchase this man's lifework, is met with the cry, "*I* buy now!" Mr. Willard is superb. The climax is perfect, the acting great, the artistic triumph indisputable.

Mr. Willard has created many notable parts, but it is doubtful whether he will ever do anything much finer than the wild outburst of scorn and triumph with which Cyrus Blenkarn meets the middleman at the moment when, half-mad with misery and failure, the crowning moment of his life comes, and all the wrong and misery, all the toil and heart-ache, all the failure and humiliation of the past years are forgotten in that one wild, exultant cry of passionate triumph. If he had done nothing else, Cyrus Blenkarn would alone entitle Mr. Willard to the gratitude of playgoers for an emotional and intellectual pleasure of a high order; and the figure of the old potter will always remain a distinct creation and a worthy achievement.

A proof of the marked individuality of the actor's style, and the crisp dialogue of Mr. Jones's plays, is afforded by the fact that upon the Parade at Brighton a short time ago an *al-fresco* elocutionist was to be heard rendering, with considerable dramatic power and a curiously clever reproduction of Mr. Willard's inflections of voice and eloquence of gesture, scenes from *The Middleman*, to a thoroughly interested audience; and the oddest part of the matter was that, in reply to the inquiry of a gentleman whose attention had been arrested as he was walking along the King's Road by what he at first believed to be Mr. Willard's voice, the humble imitator of the popular actor asserted, with every appearance of veracity, that he had acquired his knowledge of the author's text and the actor's method from only two visits to the Shaftesbury Theatre.

On April 5th a new play by Arthur Law, called *Dick Venables*, was produced at the Shaftesbury Theatre, with Mr. Willard in the title *rôle*; but the drama did not prove a popular success, nor the character of Dick Venables, a returned convict, peculiarly acceptable, although the actor contrived to introduce certain artistic touches into what was from the first an unattractive and unprofitable *rôle*. The play enjoyed but a brief life, and Mr. Willard was soon engaged upon a character offering considerably more scope for the exercise of his artistic talents.

One of the most beautiful and pathetic pieces of acting which Mr. Willard has given to the stage was his creation of the hunchback, Filippo, in Mr. Alfred Berlyn's daintily-written adaptation of François Coppée's poetical play *Le Luthier de Cremone* entitled *The Violin Makers*, produced for the first time at the Shaftesbury Theatre on April 22nd, and revived successfully on August 27th, 1890.

The sublime self-conquest of the deformed genius, who beats down the love in his own breast and foregoes a triumph as an artist in order that the girl he loves may "weep no more," but be happy with the man of her choice, his fellow-pupil, was represented by Mr. Willard with singular power and delicacy. The ecstasy of the artist; the bitter self-scorn bred of his physical infirmity; the absolute self-sacrifice; the passionate but brief spell of self-pity,—all were portrayed with true artistic feeling, and Mr. Willard's fine voice lent new music to the author's diction.

Mr. Willard has done nothing better in its way than Filippo, a most touching and beautiful impersonation, invested with an irresistible natural dignity which blots out bodily infirmity and sheds a soft light of sublime self-sacrifice which hides all physical defects, and even makes the triumph of genius, born of the brain, second to the selflessness which is the outcome of a noble nature.

Upon May 21st, 1890, the Shaftesbury Theatre was the scene of the production of a curious play—clever, daring, unconventional,—written by Mr. Henry Arthur Jones, probably with Mr. Willard in his mind as the ideal hero of a drama destined to give rise to much discussion, and to an event unique in the history of the stage—a performance given to an audience consisting entirely of the clergy. This notable play was *Judah*, and as the hero, the Rev. Judah Llewellyn, Mr. Willard found a congenial and remarkable part.

The author of *Saints and Sinners* wisely deprecated criticism of the new drama until it could be judged as a whole. For as a matter of fact, he elected to point an admirable moral by means of two acts of a most unwholesome character, and a third which went far to redeem the ill tendency of the other two.

The story was that of the loves of an earnest young Welsh Presbyterian minister, garbed like a high-church curate—presumably for æsthetic reasons—and a girl, the tool of a contemptible father, who compelled her to act the part of a hypnotic healer, and to claim supernatural powers induced by protracted fasts.

At first Vashti Dethic was worshipped by Judah Llewellyn in a purely spiritual fashion—at least so he said, and no doubt believed. She was an angel, a saint, so far above him, so pure, that the mere mention of earthly love to her was a profanation. Yet, a little later, all this spirituality was thrown to the winds at the call of passion, and the ascetic, fanatical minister, having unwillingly discovered that Vashti was an impostor, was seen to rejoice in the fact, crying that he was glad of it, as now he could make her his own; in a word, the character was transformed from a Judah to a Judas, virtually denying the spiritual in man and glorying wholly in the animal. And in this the author was to be congratulated upon his courage in preferring truth to a specious gloss of pretence. He startled and shocked—but he convinced. It was a terrible transformation, or rather a terrible revelation—but it was human nature: it was true; and therefore, as a study, to be tolerated, and, as a work of art, to be admired.

But that the first two acts of the new drama were about as unwholesome as they could be is not to be denied. They showed the audience the utter undermining of the spirituality of an intensely strong and earnest man, and the unqualified triumph of his animality, under the influence of a woman's beauty. True, this radical change was not effected without a prelude of intense agony and moral torture; true that it led to a mental and moral condition of misery that was to the man a very hell upon earth; but it meant that woman's beauty, her physical attractions and they alone, were potent enough to sweep away all moral considerations, even from a man as sublimely earnest and intensely religious as Judah Llewellyn, and to induce him to become, for the sake of the woman whose beauty had maddened him, a liar and a perjurer.

Mr. Jones displayed his knowledge of human nature in this, but whether the value of the lesson taught was worth the painful spectacle of a good man's degradation paraded without pity was a debatable point.

In the last act the author portrayed both

Judah and Vashti as worn-out by the misery of their wretched secret. There was much of the pathos of *The Scarlet Letter* in the situation, but Mr. Jones, able as he is, is not Hawthorne, and somehow or other it was not easy to feel the unmistakable thrill of sympathy either with the woman or the man. There were circumstances of sadness in her life which extenuated her career of deception; and there had been a term of living agony for the man which might well atone for his lapse from an almost superhuman height of spirituality into an abyss of lying and fierce, almost brutal, passion.

Perhaps it was just this powerful contrast which prevented the audience from feeling the full measure of sympathy which Judah was intended to command. He had been just a little too good and just a little too bad, even for poor human nature. At first Vashti was a saint and he a pious worshipper at her shrine; afterwards she was a fiend and he a reveller in her degradation, triumphing in the sin that gave her to his passion. He might love this woman with all the strength of his nature, but it was hardly necessary for him to rave of an eternity of misery to be spent together. Judah's sole virtue at one stage of the play was that he was no hypocrite. He was wholly and solely moved by the woman's beauty, and he did not pretend anything else. The climax of the last act was very fine, and almost made one condone the incidents that had gone before; and the idea of setting Judah and Vashti to work out their redemption together as man and wife, and build a church whose foundations should be Truth, was worthy and altogether beautiful. But when all was told, and the drama looked back upon calmly, it was not easy to get rid of the conviction that Mr. Jones had at last succeeded in writing an unwholesome play.

A striking, picturesque figure, Mr. Willard dominated the stage and the audience; and Judah Llewellyn, ethical considerations apart, must remain a remarkable memory with playgoers and a distinct artistic triumph for the actor.

On the afternoon of August 20th, an audience wholly composed of members of the clerical profession witnessed *Judah* by invitation, proving most appreciative, and condoning the Rev. Judah Llewellyn's lamentable lapse for the sake of Mr. E. S. Willard's consummate art.

Upon the afternoon of August 27th, 1890, Mr. Willard gave a pleasant proof of his versatility by appearing first as Filippo, in Mr. Alfred Berlyn's *The Violin Makers*, and then as Abraham Boothroyd, in a new comedy sketch, by Mr. Henry Arthur Jones, called *The Deacon*, which proved to be an amusing piece, smartly written, and virtually a defence of the stage against the prejudices of narrow-minded bigots.

As Abraham Boothroyd, wholesale bacon factor, Mayor of Chipping Padbury-on-the-Wold, and Senior Deacon of Ebenezer Chapel, grey and respectable, clad in a suit of superfine black, with pale face, square grey beard, and long, clean-shaven, rigid upper lip—a monument of prosperous piety and middle-class respectability, and a bundle of deeply-rooted prejudices, Mr Willard was irresistible. Little tradesmanlike tricks of manner, a faint North-country burr in the rich voice, a quiet twinkle in the eye as if the old Adam were not wholly dead, and just the right note of passing pathos here and there, necessary to give the man a certain dignity, proved Mr. Willard a close observer of human nature.

Coming to London to take part in an indignation meeting to rescue Exeter Hall from the contamination of being converted into a theatre, he is taken to a theatre instead, and is himself converted from his prejudices with a rather miraculous suddenness and completeness, partly by the discovery that the Juliet who has awakened such tender memories in his old heart is the child of his own daughter, who had run away from home with an actor twenty years before.

The Deacon was only what it professed to be, a sketch, but it was so smartly written, and, above all, it gave Mr. Willard a *rôle* so rich in quiet comedy, that Abraham Boothroyd ranked at once as a distinct creation, and a pleasant addition to the *répertoire* of the actor.

After a brief but very successful farewell appearance in the provinces, Mr. Willard set out for America on October 18th, 1890, seeking new laurels in a land where other notable players from the old country had found so warm a welcome, and followed by hearty goodwill and sympathetic interest on the part of thousands of English playgoers, who had long ago learned to recognise in him one of the foremost, ablest, most capable, and most conscientious players of the period.

It was characteristic of Mr. Willard's strong sympathy for everything Shakespearean that on the last Sunday spent in England before his departure for the States, after playing in Birmingham on the Saturday night, he made a pilgrimage from Kenilworth to Warwick, and then to Stratford-on-Avon with Mr. Howard Paul and another friend, dining at the old "Red Horse," upon the very table on which Washington Irving wrote his delightful sketch of the old town in which Shakespeare was born. It is not difficult to believe that as the popular actor "lolled back in his elbow-chair, and cast a complacent look about the little parlour of the Red Horse," that "the words of sweet Shakespeare" passed through his mind as they had passed many years before through that of the brilliant author of the inimitable "Sketch-book."

Mr. Willard opened in New York at Palmer's Theatre, on November 10th, in *The Middleman*, and at once secured a complete success, his impersonation of Cyrus Blenkarn being accepted by critics and public alike as a thoroughly artistic and convincing creation, and that initial performance was the first step upon a tour through America which proved one continuous series of successes. Mr. Willard's peculiarly earnest and straightforward style of acting, combined with the elaborate and thoroughly artistic finish of his characterisation, took the American audiences by storm, and they accepted him at once and without question. That he should so speedily win favour on the other side of the Atlantic is not surprising to those who know the mood of the best-class audiences in the United States. There is a shrewness and natural keenness of judgment about them not altogether unlike that which characterises north-country audiences here, with whom, too, Mr. Willard is extremely popular. But when all is said, the sufficient reason for his Transatlantic success may be found in the artistic conception and conscientious study which Mr. Willard brings to bear upon every *rôle* which he undertakes, whether in the Old World or the New.

*I don't pretend to
be a particularly
good sort of fellow —
nor a particularly
bad sort of fellow.*
Caste. Act I.

S. B. BANCROFT.

BY a happy conjunction of circumstances, Mr. S. B. Bancroft has achieved a position of peculiar interest in the chronicles of the contemporary stage. A clever and conscientious actor, he might yet have not bulked so largely in the eye of the world, had it not been that, in conjunction with the late T. W. Robertson, he created a new *genus* of dramatic character, and, more than that, reflected with unimpeachable fidelity the physical, mental, and moral peculiarities of a numerous body of men about town. Mr. Bancroft achieved the sublimation of the British swell, and forged a new and lasting link between society and the stage.

The combined tenderness of the author and refinement of the actor, enabled the *genus* "swell" to recognise in the dramatic mirror a somewhat flattering portrait of itself, learning, perhaps to its surprise, that a man-about-town might have a heart, and a "heavy swell" be not wholly void of brain. This titillated the *amour propre* of the class which gave the dramatist such types as Jack Poyntz, Captain Hawtree, and Sir Frederick Blount, and ensured the success of the actor. Mr. Bancroft presented a section of society—and a section with as much influence to-day as it had when, as the late Lord Lamington told in the delightful reminiscences which Death killed all too soon, George IV. gave his famous breakfast to conciliate "the dandies" of whom the "Bancroft swells" are the legitimate descendants—with its portrait. And if by the exercise of their art the author and the actor invested the counterfeit presentments with perhaps a rather more generous share of lovable and manly attributes than Nature commonly bestows upon the living originals, the excess was kindly, diplomatic, easily condonable.

The one great charm about Mr. Bancroft's most notable creations, or, if not the most notable, at least those with which he is most generally identified, was that they were essentially gentlemen. They might not scintillate with intellectuality, their brains might not always be as brilliant as their boots, they might not be free from many weaknesses of will and wit; but they had the instincts of gentlemen. One felt that they were in the main honest, loyal, scorning a lie or any mean thing, reverencing, if in somewhat easy-going fashion, their conscience as their king; and, although perhaps a little dense and apt to blunder off the line now and again, for the most part holding a very clear code of honour—a code which might not always square with the notions of *bourgeois* respectability and convention, but Draconian in its claim upon their conscience, and rendering impossible any mean or cruel thing.

Society of to-day is not wholly lacking in Colonel Newcomes, but, for one *preux chevalier* of that exquisitely perfect type, there are hundreds of Jack Poyntzes, of Blounts, of

Hawtrees—good, slow-witted, but big-hearted fellows, who, to paraphrase Rochester on Charles II., "never do a cruel thing and rarely say a wise one," but who yet inspire confidence and affection by their simple manliness and dunderheaded but dogged honesty. And this numerous class looked in the mirror which Mr. Bancroft held up to nature, saw themselves at their best, and, pardonably enough, did not quickly weary of contemplating the pleasant picture.

There can be no doubt that the satisfying completeness with which Mr. Bancroft idealised the "heavy swell" went straight to the heart of society, and compelled success. It is especially true of the actor's calling that "those who live to please must please to live," and Mr. Bancroft's creations were above all things pleasant—clean, wholesome, refined, good-hearted types of English gentlemen, whose foibles and harmless affectations it was possible to laugh at without an atom of contempt. Indeed, the more one laughed at them the more one loved them—they were so very human, and their little tincture of absurdity was distinctly consolatory to all who are wise enough to recognise that the profoundest philosopher, the most dignified personage, is not without his humorous side to the acute student of human nature.

Nor, when occasion served, did Mr. Bancroft fail to indicate, with a good deal of quiet power, the pluck, the dignity, the chivalrous loyalty and almost womanly tenderness which help to make up the best type of manhood. Without this his art would have been incomplete and unsatisfying, for had he merely shown the glittering surface of society life, and failed to reveal the strongly running undercurrent of earnestness and forceful emotions, he might speedily have wearied the public and worn out his welcome. Beneath the surface-nonchalance, the lip-cynicism or banality, the apparent shallowness of the man-of-the-world, would all at once be indicated unsuspected depths of feeling, fierce passions kept in check by an iron will, beautiful brotherly tenderness, ardent love of man for woman, all that go to make a complete man and perfect gentleman; and the actor's talent proved itself versatile, and vigorous, faithful, analytic and convincing.

To create a distinct school of character, and to invest a difficult and often dull type of man with some humour, and a real, but often unsuspected worthiness and charm, were no mean achievements, and Mr. Bancroft would have fairly earned the reputation he enjoys had he done nothing more than this; but, like all successful actors, his *répertoire* has been as varied as its range was wide.

It was on January 1st, 1861, as Mr. Bancroft records in that interesting volume of reminiscences, "Mr. and Mrs. Bancroft On and Off the Stage," that he, a stage-stricken youth, plodded along the cheerless streets of Birmingham to the Theatre Royal, where he was engaged by Mr. Mercer Simpson at the modest salary of a guinea a week, to play whatever might be thrown in his way. And, a few nights later, he made his first appearance upon any stage in the humble guise of a courtier in the pantomime, hiding his feelings whatever they may have been, behind a comic mask.

Whatever success or the reverse attained

by the *débutant* in this initial part was so impersonal, thanks to the mask, that it is not recorded, but the assumption is that the "courtier" showed some glimmer of light through the chinks of his bushel, as, immediately after, he was entrusted with his first speaking part, that of Lieutenant Manley, in Mr. Bayle Bernard's drama *St. Mary's Eve*.

Evidently the juvenile enthusiast showed even then some promise of his future excellence, for, during the season, which came to an end in July, Mr. Bancroft enacted no less than thirty-six different parts, appearing, among other things, with Madame Celeste in those old-fashioned dramas *The Green Bushes* and *Flowers of the Forest*.

Then followed a term of provincial apprenticeship, which must have proved invaluable as a means of training the memory and giving elasticity to the mind by imposing upon the young actor a constantly changing round of more or less responsible impersonations. The work must have been onerous and incessant, but it was congenial, and "the labour we delight in physics pain," while the zealous young recruit, anxious to rise from the ranks as rapidly as might be, welcomed what under other circumstances might have appeared intolerable drudgery.

After the close of his first season in Dublin, Mr. Bancroft fulfilled a brief engagement in Cork, returning to Birmingham for the season terminating in the spring of 1862, by which period he had mastered sixty-four new parts. Then came a few weeks' engagement in the summer at Devonport, where for the first time he played leading parts,. the first being that of Captain Murphy Maguire in *The Serious Family*, and the other that of Captain Hawkesley in *Still Waters run Deep*.

The remainder of 1862 and the years 1863 and 1864 were occupied by a short engagement in Birmingham ; a season in Dublin, during which, in the spring of 1863, Mr. Bancroft received an offer to join the company of the St. James's Theatre, but preferred to increase his experience in the provinces before facing a London audience ; a month's engagement in Birmingham, followed by a successful summer in Devonport, during which an offer, again declined, was made for him to go to the Princess's Theatre ; a return to Dublin in 1864, and then an engagement at the Prince of Wales's, Liverpool, where Mr. Bancroft met Miss Marie Wilton for the first time, and accepted an engagement to join the company which she was forming to open the Prince of Wales's Theatre in Tottenham Court Road, in conjunction with Mr. H. J. Byron.

With the Liverpool engagement Mr. Bancroft's provincial wanderings came to an end, but that he owed much to the wide experience gained during that laborious period of four years and four months is obvious from the fact that during that time he played no less than three hundred and forty-six parts, covering almost every conceivable detail of dramatic work.

Remembering this, it is perhaps all the more remarkable that Mr. Bancroft should so quickly and so completely become identified with a class of character new to the stage, and of conspicuous individuality of style.

Happily, the author of the series of delightful plays which founded what has been called with flippant injustice the teacup-and-saucer school of comedy, was no believer in the cynical theory that

> "To feel for none is the true social art
> Of the world's stoics—men without a heart."

His men of the world might be stoical in so far as a repression of any outward sign of strong feeling, whether of joy or suffering, was concerned. But for all their Spartan or, it might be, Sybaritic self-sufficiency, they were creatures of living flesh and blood, in whom the pulses of human passions throbbed with no less strength because good breeding and caste traditions forbade hysterical and violent manifestations.

The opening of the Prince of Wales's Theatre, from which Mr. Bancroft's record as a metropolitan actor dates, took place on Saturday, April 15th, 1865, with a piece called *A Winning Hazard* by Mr. J. P. Wooler, in which Mr. Bancroft made his first appearance on a London stage, and an operatic burlesque extravaganza, called *La! Sonnambula! or, The Supper, the Sleeper, and the Merry Swiss Boy;* "being a passage in the life of a famous 'Woman in White,' a passage leading to a tip-top story, told in this instance by Henry J. Byron." The programme, which was then commonly of the three-decker description, was completed by the farce of *Vandyke Brown*.

In May Mr. Bancroft appeared in a comic drama by Palgrave Simpson, called *A Fair Pretender*, and on June 10th he created the *rôle* of Captain Thistleton, in H. J. Byron's bright and successful comedy, *War to the Knife*. In this clever play Mr. Bancroft impersonated the man-about-town with much of the quiet humour and originality which were afterwards to be employed to so much advantage, and attracted an amount of favourable notice which fairly started him upon a career of popularity and success.

On September 25th, 1865, Mr. Bancroft assumed with renewed success the principal part in Dion Boucicault's farce, *A Lover by Proxy*, and it was on November 11th in the same year that the keynote of the subsequent career of Mr. Bancroft, and the lady who was soon to become his wife, was struck by the production of the first of the series of charming Robertsonian comedies, *Society*.

Although the piece had been played with success in Liverpool, it was not approached without some qualms and misgivings, naturally exaggerated by the feeling that so much depended upon its finding favour with the somewhat exacting and exceptional *habitués* of the Prince of Wales's Theatre. But courage conquered, the piece was produced, and all the best people flocked to see themselves satirised, and to laugh good-naturedly at their own foibles —no doubt thinking all the while how excellently the cap fitted their dearest friends. Upon the first representation of *Society* Mr. Bancroft was cast for Sidney Daryl, and the managerial acumen which entrusted him with so responsible a part was justified by its skilful rendition. Later, when the comedy was revived, with gratifying success, on September 21st, 1868, Mr. Bancroft appeared as Tom Stylus, and presented a curious but not uncommon phase of Bohemian character with remarkable fidelity and much shrewd humour.

In Mr. Byron's comedy, *A Hundred Thousand Pounds*, produced on May 5th, 1866, Mr. Bancroft created the part of General Gerald Goodwin, and then appeared with the Prince of Wales's company in Liverpool, when, in addition to the existing *répertoire*, the new comedy *Ours*, by T. W. Robertson, was given a trial trip, before being launched upon the wider waters of metropolitan criticism.

It was on September 15th, 1866, that *Ours* was first produced at the Prince of Wales's Theatre, with immediate and unqualified success. Mr. Bancroft created the *rôle* of Angus Macalister with all the care and finish which playgoers had by this time learned to expect from an actor who was obviously and always conscientious. He played the new part for an unbroken run of a hundred and fifty nights, and consolidated his claim upon the good opinion of the public.

As Captain Hawtree, in *Caste*, the next of the famous Robertsonian series, produced at the Prince of Wales's Theatre on April 6th, 1867, Mr. Bancroft was perfectly in his element. It is not difficult to imagine how easily the character might have been vulgarised, or else conventionalised into a comparative nonentity. An over-dressed, swaggering, noisy Hawtree might have been evolved from the inner consciousness of a commonplace character-actor, but in the hands of Mr. Bancroft the author's ideal was safe. The make-up alone was a consummate piece of art. Quietly dressed, as the heavy dragoon school of swells like Hawtree are always sure to be; with sleek, dark hair, and all the personal characteristics of a well-groomed man, this new style of stage fop came as a revelation to those accustomed to more coarsely-painted portraits of a class not easily imitated or, in truth, generally understood; but it was so convincing in its quiet realism that it was accepted without hesitation, and welcomed as a notable addition to dramatic types. The drawling speech and apparent affectation, the stolid solemnity relieved by a subtly suggested shrewdness, the "good form" of the man with it all, his slight *soupçon* of horsiness, the whole tone of the creation—were irresistible; and the actor's reputation became more firmly rooted than ever. The piece ran right through the season, which ended in July, and was then played in Liverpool and Manchester with equal success.

The odour of popularity in which *Caste* was steeped when the end of the season arrived enabled Mrs. Bancroft to revive the play with renewed success when the autumn campaign commenced, on September 28th, 1867, and it was not until December 21st that Mr. Bancroft was afforded an opportunity of creating one more " swell "—there is no other word which conveys the idea of his impersonations so clearly and completely—in the *rôle* of Beecher Sprawley, in Dion Boucicault's comedy *How She Loves Him*, in which the actor once more pleased playgoers and won new commendation from the critics, although the play itself, despite much clever dialogue and some supremely amusing situations, only ran forty-seven nights.

When the new comedy by T. W. Robertson, called *Play*, was produced, on the night of Saturday, February 15th, 1868, Mr. Bancroft was provided with the *rôle* of an unmitigated rascal and impudent adventurer, in which he exhibited his talent to great advantage, and the Chevalier Browne proved one more succesful and notable addition to his *répertoire*. This was followed by another revival of *Caste*, which lasted until the close of the season on July 27th, the theatre being then closed until September 21st, when *Society* was revived, Mr. Bancroft then taking the part of Tom Stylus with admirable effect, his nonchalant air suiting the character to perfection.

On December 12th a new comedy by Mr. Edmund Yates, *Tame Cats*, was produced, Mr. Bancroft appearing as Mortimer Wedgwood, a poet-charlatan and "tame cat" of a class that did not commend itself to the public taste, and the play only ran for eleven nights, being followed by a revival of the ever-popular *Society;* and on January 16th, 1869, the new Robertsonian comedy, *School*, was produced with instant and unqualified success, Mr. Bancroft creating the delightfully sympathetic part of Jack Poyntz with admirable art, revelling in the quiet humour of the character to the utmost, and presenting, too, an excellent picture of the well-bred lover, handsome, well-groomed, well-tailored, and an altogether wholesome and agreeable specimen of Young England.

School was an enormous success, running right through the season, and being revived again on September 11th, to crowded houses; being played altogether three hundred and eighty-one times.

The last comedy destined to be written for the Prince of Wales's Theatre by the pen that had done so much worthy work was produced on April 23rd, 1870, and *M.P.* proved at once as pronounced a success as any of its predecessors, Mr. Bancroft exhibiting, in the *rôle* of Talbot Piers, his customary shrewdness, self-control, and quiet humour. An autumn revival was followed by a revival of *Ours* on

MR. BANCROFT AS JACK POYNTZ IN "SCHOOL."

November 26th, Mr. Bancroft then taking the part of Hugh Chalcot, instead of his original one of Angus Macalister, and acquitting himself to the complete satisfaction of author and audience. The revival ran through the following season with unbroken success, to be followed in its turn by a revival of *Caste* in September 1871, and a production of *Money* on May 4th, 1872, with Mr. Bancroft as Sir Frederick Blount, an admirable piece of acting, remarkable for the refinement and distinction with which the actor invested this and similar parts—the physically colourless and mentally inane baronet, with his lisp, his drawl, his vacuous stare and excellently-cut clothes, being perfect in his peculiar way.

It was not until February 22nd, 1873, that it became advisable to supersede Lord Lytton's comedy with Mr. Wilkie Collins's adaptation of his powerful novel *Man and Wife*, in which Mr. Bancroft undertook the minor part of Mr. Speedwell, a doctor, but made it of value by thoughtful and refined acting.

A revival of *School* followed, on September 20th, 1873, with Mr. Bancroft as Jack Poyntz, and so great was its success that it was not until April 4th, 1874, that *The School for Scandal* was acted for the first time by the Prince of Wales's company, Mr. Bancroft proving an unconventional Joseph Surface, his studious moderation and careful avoidance of an overemphasis of the objectionable characteristics of the man being purely artistic, and rendering the *rôle* natural and acceptable to a rare degree, Joseph's villainy being indicated rather than expressed, with a *finesse* and delicacy infinitely more effective than any bolder or coarser interpretation could have been. The actor seemed thoroughly imbued with the spirit of the age in which the action is laid, wore the picturesque dress with grace, and expressed the superficial courtliness of the manners of the period with much lucidity and distinction, his Joseph Surface being to the full as clever an assumption as his affected macaroni Sir Benjamin Backbite, in a *matinée* revival of the old comedy given on May 14th, 1870, at Drury Lane, for the benefit of the Dramatic College.

Mr. Bancroft modestly contented himself with the small part of the Prince of Morocco in the notable Prince of Wales's revival of *The Merchant of Venice*, on April 17th, 1875, contriving, as with everything else he touched, to endue it with a certain importance. Admirably as the play was mounted, and, for the most part, acted, it only held the stage for thirty-six performances, to be succeeded by a revival of *Money*, and on June 19th Mr. Bancroft proved his comedy power again at a *matinée* performance of Mr. Honeyton in Theyre Smith's delightful comedietta *A Happy Pair*.

Mr. Bancroft's next impersonation of importance revealed a pathos and a power of which many of those who had only seen him in Robertsonian comedy did not suspect him capable, and compelled playgoers to recognise in him something beyond and better than an absolutely modern school actor, capable only of representing types of his own world and period. Triplet, in the Prince of Wales's revival of *Masks and Faces* on November 5th, 1875, proved one of the most artistic pieces of work yet done by the actor. Mr. Bancroft's thoughtful and delicate method was brought to bear with delightful effect upon the representation

MR. BANCROFT AS "TRIPLET" IN "MASKS AND FACES."

of the pathetic, beautiful figure of the half-starved musician—so tender, so exquisitely refined in every instinct, with so great a heart, so sensitive a soul in his bowed and shrunken frame—and the result was a Triplet of rare tenderness and dignity, with whom one laughed the kindliest laugh of all, that which is born while sympathetic tears are in the eyes. In a sense this was the most valuable part Mr. Bancroft had as yet essayed before a London audience, as its artistic possibilities were so great, and it was all the more gratifying that he developed these potentialities to the utmost under the difficult condition of being handicapped by identification with a class of characters which, in their faultlessly-dressed, well-fed, languid, nonchalant nineteenth-century swelldom, formed the most vivid contrast to the pinched, threadbare dignity of the shabby broken-down gentleman—author, actor, and artist—whose ill-starred fortunes could not mar his innate sweetness and artistic refinement of character, and who could be tender with his sick wife and tolerant of his noisy crew of children, while his own heart was bruised and aching and sick with hope deferred well-nigh to the point of despair. Mr. Bancroft's Triplet was profoundly moving, the half-broken heart pulsing in every tone of the voice, and the forced smiles and hysterical gaiety, infinitely sadder than tears, revealing the nature and condition of the man with an art as delicate as it was convincing and complete.

On Thursday, April 13th, 1876, Mr. Bancroft appeared as Bob Blewitt, in Byron's ill-fated piece *Wrinkles*, speaking countless smart things with admirable humour; but the play only ran eighteen nights, and was followed by a revival of *Ours*.

In *Peril*, an excellent adaptation of Sardou's *Nos Intimes*, by Messrs. B. C. Stephenson and Clement Scott, the first adaptation from the French produced at the Prince of Wales's Theatre under the management of Mr. and Mrs. Bancroft, Mr. Bancroft figured to advantage as Sir George Ormond, and in the crucial scene with his wife he was manly, tender, and in every respect the *beau idéal* of an English gentleman. The production was a great success, and although it was first given on September 30th, 1876, it was not until March 31st, 1877, that Mr. Bancroft appeared as Dazzle in a production of *London Assurance*—a most admirable piece of acting, full of devil-may-care impudence, and quite one of the best things he had done.

From September 29th, until the end of the year Mr. Bancroft appeared as Blenkinsop in Tom Taylor's comedy *An Unequal Match*, and on Saturday, January 12th, 1878, he created with immense success the *rôle* of Count Orloff in *Diplomacy*, the English adaptation of Sardou's *Dora*, by Messrs B. C. Stephenson and Clement Scott. In the part of Count Orloff, Mr. Bancroft had one magnificent opportunity for the exhibition of that "reserved force" and indicated rather than expressed emotion which is one of the most conspicuous and admirable features of his dramatic method; and in the great *scène des trois hommes*, which is the crucial point of the play, he acted with a quiet power, a perfectly

MR. BANCROFT AS COUNT ORLOFF IN "DIPLOMACY."

modulated passion, which were the perfection of art, and stamped him once and for all as an actor of the first rank. Mr. Bancroft succeeded in completely merging his own strongly marked personality in that of the Russian Count, and made a conspicuous success with a minimum of opportunity in a part which he himself prefers to any of his impersonations.

On January 11th, 1879, Mr. Bancroft resumed his impersonation of Captain Hawtree, in a revival of *Caste*, and towards the end of the season appeared successfully as Harry Spreadbrow and Sir Henry Spreadbrow in Mr. W. S. Gilbert's dainty little idyl *Sweethearts*, one of the tenderest, prettiest prose-poems in the literature of the English stage; and subsequently as Harry Collier in *Good for Nothing*.

Before leaving the Prince of Wales's Theatre for the Haymarket, Mr. Bancroft reappeared as Hugh Chalcot in a revival of *Ours*, and the familiar but perennially popular play sufficed to make the final season a success.

It was on Saturday, January 31st, 1880, that Mr. and Mrs. Bancroft entered upon their tenancy of the Haymarket Theatre, and revived in excellent style Lord Lytton's comedy *Money*, Mr. Bancroft resuming his part of the flaxen-haired Sir Frederick Blount. The occasion was notable for more reasons than one, the abolition of the pit by the new management giving rise to a serious disturbance when the curtain went up, which lasted for twenty minutes, and had to be faced not by Mr. Bancroft *in propria personâ*, but by Sir Frederick Blount, who, despite his effeminate, foppish outside, proved by his admirable imperturbability and patience that he had the making of a man in him after all. The play itself was entirely successful, and filled the theatre until the revival, on May 1st, of *School*, with Mr. Bancroft in his original part. In November the successful run of *School* was resumed, and Mr. Bancroft also appeared as Mr. George Clarke, C. B., the travelled bachelor, in *The Vicarage*; and on February 5th, 1881, *Masks and Faces* was revived, Mr. Bancroft alternating his touching and delicate study of Triplet with a carefully elaborated and amusing impersonation of Colley Cibber.

The Haymarket revival of Tom Taylor's *Plot and Passion*, on November 26th, 1881, was not too successful, but Mr. Bancroft's rendering of Joseph Fouché, Duke of Otranto, was admitted to be an artistic and finished conception of the part; and on January 19th, 1882, he resumed his arduous *rôle* of Hugh Chalcot in the revival of *Ours*, in which Mrs. Langtry commenced her first series of appearances as a professional actress.

On Tuesday, April 25th, 1882, the English version of Sardou's *Odette* was produced in a most elaborate way, and proved an instant success, Mr. Bancroft giving force and distinction to the *rôle* of Lord Henry Trevene, and adding a notable figure to his catalogue of dramatic creations.

Tom Taylor's comedy *The Overland Route* was produced at the Haymarket on October 7th, 1882, with Mr. Bancroft as Tom Dexter, in which character he again won the favour of the public; and the year 1883 found the player in his old part of Captain Hawtree in a revival of *Caste*, on January 20th, the final performance of which, on April 13th, was the occasion of a quite remarkable demonstration on the part of a crowded audience. A final brief revival of *School* followed, and on May 5th Mr. Herman Merivale's version of Sardou's *Fédora* was produced, with immense success, Mr. Bancroft giving a polished and well thought out rendering of Jean de Siriex, a French diplomatist, his *distingué* style standing him in good stead in a *rôle* demanding personal qualifications of a high order. The resumption of the piece on September 29th was attended by a circumstance which lent it peculiar interest. Mr. Bancroft assumed for the first time the *rôle* of Count Loris Ipanoff, and there was considerable curiosity to see how he would acquit himself in a part directly opposed to the class of character with which he was identified. Those who were familiar with the lights and shades of Mr. Bancroft's acting were tolerably sanguine that his new impersonation would be a success, and the event justified their confidence, for, if there were some faults in Mr. Bancroft's new assumption, there were also flashes of brilliant acting which fully atoned for them.

The impression conveyed by Mr. Bancroft's appearance, voice, and gestures in the earlier scenes was that, probably unintentionally, possibly unconsciously, he was reproducing some of the mannerisms of another distinguished player—the melodramatic stride, the peculiar inflexion and studied hoarseness of the voice, and certain tricks of hand and head, having apparently strayed from the neighbourhood of the Strand to the stage of the Haymarket. But, as he warmed to his work, Mr. Bancroft threw off these peculiarities, and displayed the power which he had in reserve. Throughout the second act Mr. Bancroft was good, but in the third he was something more—his delineation of passion, despair, a wild desire for vengeance, and an absorbing love, being a masterly piece of acting. In a drama like *Fédora*, where everything is so highly pitched, and where the passion is so intense as to at times appear unnatural, the over-accentuation of any detail may prove an element of grave danger, and once or twice Mr. Bancroft ventured perilously near the boundary which divides the sublime from the ridiculous; but he grasped so completely and portrayed with such consummate ability the intense passion and agony of the situation, that his Loris Ipanoff was justly accepted as one of his most artistic successes.

When Mr. Pinero's clever, curious comedy, *Lords and Commons*, was produced at the Haymarket on November 14th, 1883, Mr. Bancroft, made up in remarkable fashion with a long orange-hued beard, was scarcely recognised at first in the character of Tom Jervoise; but the actor's voice and manner soon revealed his identity, and he received a cordial welcome, quickly justified by his admirable acting in the part.

After a successful run of eighty nights, *Lords and Commons* gave place to a revival of *Peril*, with Mr. Bancroft as Dr. Thornton, a *rôle* acted with energy and a shrewd perception of the possibilities of the part, which he developed to the uttermost.

On May 3rd, 1884, *The Rivals* was revived, with Mr. Bancroft as Faulkland, and ran with some success.

The farewell season was devoted chiefly to

the revival of plays in which Mr. Bancroft and his brilliant wife had won popular success.

Perhaps the most notable of these, inasmuch as Mr. Bancroft appeared for the first time as Henry Beauclerc instead of Count Orloff, was that of *Diplomacy*, on November 8th, 1884, the distinction and *autorité* demanded by such a *rôle* being manifested by Mr. Bancroft with a quiet force which few other living actors could have brought to bear upon a part calling for certain very special and rare qualities. The manner and bearing of the new Henry Beauclerc —diplomat, polished man of the world, kindly elder brother, lenient critic of poor humanity— were perfect, inspiring a regard and esteem, even a confidence and affection, which made it easy to understand the influence which men of that calibre can and do exert with unobtrusive but resistless force.

Not even the epidemic of Russophobia current at the time, however, combined with the admirable acting of Mr. and Mrs. Bancroft, sufficed to galvanise *Ours* into a great success on the occasion of its revival in April 1885, the episodes which in the old days were received with enthusiasm failing to arouse any marked degree of interest, and the weakness of the Shendryn sub-plot, and the ridiculous improbability of the hut scene in the Crimea, in which—waiving the unlikelihood of such a foregathering—we see women who have fainted with emotion at the mere departure of the troops indulging in pantomimic antics with curious levity upon the actual battle-field, seemed more obtrusive than usual. But the revival certainly served to remind the public that in Mr. Bancroft they would soon lose a capable actor, whose place it would be hard to fill, for in Hugh Chalcot he again gave a most admirable study of a man whose sole affliction in life is literally an *embarras de richesses*. The imperturbable *sang-froid*, the dry humour, with just sufficient cynicism to make it piquant without veiling the good-nature of the man, the quaint lamentations over his wealth, the delight of finding a woman who loved him for himself, were brought out to perfection, and new reason was given for playgoers to regret the impending loss of an actor whose powers were ripening to such perfection.

But the farewell night, July 20th, 1885, proved beyond all doubt the high position which Mr. Bancroft had secured in the opinion of the playgoing public. The Prince and Princess of Wales and a great representative crowd of London society gathered together to do honour to Mr. and Mrs. Bancroft, and the occasion proved one to be long memorable in the annals of the stage; while the programme comprised the names of a remarkable company of representative actors and actresses. Mr. Bancroft appeared in his exquisitely pathetic *rôle* of Triplet, with Mrs. Bancroft as Peg Woffington, and subsequently delivered with admirable effect a farewell address, and " Valedictory Ode," conceived by Mr. Clement Scott with excellent taste.

After so definitive a farewell to the stage as that taken by Mr. and Mrs. Bancroft upon that memorable night, the playgoing public learned with some surprise that upon the occasion of the revival of *The Dead Heart* at the Lyceum, on October 28th, 1889, the *rôle* of the Abbé Latour would be undertaken by Mr. Bancroft. The rumour was at first received with some incredulity, but, to the satisfaction of playgoers, it proved to be well founded, and in due course they had the pleasure of giving a cordial welcome to an old favourite whom they had scarcely hoped to see again.

Possibly the warmth of his reception, and the knowledge that a great deal would be expected of him, combined with a comparative strangeness to the ordeal of the footlights which so prolonged an absence had involved, shook the actor's nerve, for at first his Abbé was not completely satisfying. The callous, cynical man of the world was there, polished and refined as Mr. Bancroft knew so well how to make him, but for a while there was too much repose, a too persistent painting of the character in monochrome, a plentiful lack of animation. Beneath the imperturbable surface it was not difficult for the critical few to discern all the fierce hate, cynical falseness, and patrician courage of the man; but to a superficial observer the Abbé seemed at first but a colourless creation of only moderate interest.

But when the actor had got acclimatised

once more to the enervating atmosphere of stage-land, all his old talent was perceptible. With many a subtle touch he made the Abbé an embodiment of aristocratic disdain, refined villainy, heartless cynicism, absolute self-love, while in the great duel scene he evolved a power, a *finesse*, a splendid courage which took the house by storm, and redeemed whatever weakness might have preceded it. From first to last the impersonation was marked by refinement and distinction, and in the duel scene it rose to the height of tragedy,—the moment in which he dragged the handkerchief, stained with blood, from his breast, being just one of those touches which remain in the memory, and compel an audience to recognise the presence of talent of a very high order. That one tragic episode, combined with the passionate intensity of the whole of the duel scene, and the perfect refinement of the conception and rendition of the part throughout, rendered Mr. Bancroft's Latour a notable impersonation, and his return to the stage the subject of general congratulation.

Mr. Bancroft is very popular off the stage, and his charming house in Berkeley Square is the scene of much pleasant hospitality, both Mr. Bancroft and his clever wife thoroughly understanding the art of entertaining their guests to perfection. Mr. Bancroft's judgment, in all matters connected with his profession, is so highly valued that, on more than one occasion, he has acted successfully as arbitrator between dramatic authors and managers who could not agree as to the acceptance or rejection of dramas ; and his ready wit was amusingly exemplified in a romantic dispute in the law courts in 1881, when he was summoned as a witness and questioned as to what could or could not terminate the run of a piece. The following little specimen of a word-duel is worthy of the stage :—

COUNSEL.—" But supposing your leading actress was injured coming down to the theatre, you would be compelled to close the doors ? "

MR. BANCROFT.—" Such a thing would be impossible in a well-conducted theatre."

COUNSEL.—" How so ? "

MR. BANCROFT.—" She would be understudied."

COUNSEL (*a happy thought*).—"But supposing

by some miracle the under-study was in the same cab with her and both were injured: what then?"

MR. BANCROFT (*unabashed*).—" I should send on the Prompter!"

This absolute imperturbability is distinctly characteristic of the popular actor, and has had not a little to do with his pronounced and persistent success, " on and off the stage."

JOHN LAWRENCE TOOLE.

MOST men are born babies, but Mr. Toole must have been born a comedian. It is not absolutely on record that he made puns between his spoonfuls of pap, or lisped out a request for a comic wig in preference to waiting for Nature to do her work in her own way, but the late Edward Laman Blanchard used to delight in telling how, in the course of a country walk, as long ago as the year 1838, he chanced upon a small boy of five or six years old, who, having been sent into pastures new for his health, had so speedily acquired a sense of "local colour," that he was entertaining a select audience of other small folk with a series of quite wonderful imitations of farmyard birds and animals, with humorously interjected human voices, the mimetic power displayed auguring well for the future talent of the precocious performer, Master Johnny Toole.

The son of a City toast-master, and accustomed, in the intervals of consuming infantile portions of those items in the *menu* which represent the sweetness and light of lordly banquets in the civic halls, to study human nature from the cosy security of a screened corner or quiet gallery, John Lawrence Toole had ample opportunity for storing up in his receptive and reproductive mind a host of odd impressions, to be used in after years with excellent effect; and when, as a youth, he relieved his diurnal labours at "the desk's dead wood" in the office of a wine-merchant by nocturnal performances as an amateur actor at Sussex Hall, Leadenhall Street, as a member of the City Histrionic Club, his love of acting rapidly developed into a ruling passion, only to be fully gratified at last by the adoption of the stage as a career; and his resolve, made nearly forty years ago, has afforded an incalculable amount of innocent pleasure to tens of thousands of people, while no doubt the comedian has himself been happier than had he become ever so rich and famous as the proprietor of "Toole's Griffin B Sherry" or celebrated "Guildhall Port" at twenty-four shillings a dozen—bottles included.

Whimsicality, quaintness, and a boldness of delineation which sometimes breaks through the boundary which divides character-drawing from caricature, have been the dominant elements in Mr. Toole's acting as long as playgoers of the period can remember. His artistic method is to the stage not wholly unlike that associated in the popular mind with the name of George Cruikshank in another field of art. In the works of both, especially when Mr. Toole's creations are judged simply as stage figures and estimated for their pictile quality, there is much the same freehanded treatment, much the same inoffensive *grotesquerie*, much the same whimsical exaggeration of characteristic features of physique and dress.

But exaggeration is not without its value in either the art of the worker with the pencil and the brush, or of the actor who uses his very self to body forth his idea of a character.

The caricaturist, on or off the stage, if he be of the first rank, recognises the imperative axiom that it is the business of his peculiar method to heighten, not to disfigure or destroy, the individuality of a subject, and it is indisputable that in the case of George Cruikshank and of John Lawrence Toole each has made his creations the more striking and memorable by this artistic and legitimate utilisation of exaggeration. Cruikshank's Artful Dodger or Fagin, and Toole's Caleb Plummer or Dodger or Dick Dolland, exhibit very much the same degree of exaggeration, and it is unquestionable that all the figures make a far clearer and more enduring impression than would have been possible had the artist or the actor permitted himself to be strictly trammelled by the limits of actuality. But with both, too, there was always one clearly apparent condition—the original conception upon which they worked was based upon a keen and true insight into human nature. Without that they might have explored the artistic field from Dan to Beersheba, and still it would have proved barren of worthy fruit.

Mr. Toole, moreover, is an actor of no mean versatility. He has not yet, it is true, given to the stage a new Hamlet or an ideal Romeo; sentiment and romance of the higher or of the more conventional school are not within his range; neither for him is the passion or despair of pure tragedy. But in the field of domestic life and every-day joys and sorrows he is a thorough master of his art, and is equally effective with the *piano* pedal of pathos hard down as with the *forte* of boisterous farce. He can make his audience laugh with him and weep with him at will, and, even in his broadest and wildest farcical extravagances, while they roar at his comic bewilderment, for very good-fellowship they wish him well out of his scrapes.

Mr. Toole is a thorough comedian and *bon camarade*, through and through, hence his extreme popularity in the profession and with the public. He is not cast in the heroic mould, but very little of the downright useful work of the world is done by heroes, and so it is with the drama. Who shall compute the pleasure given and pure sympathy evoked by Mr. Toole in his comical and pathetic moments; and although he may not have attained the dignity of a Charles I., the intellectual, melancholy charm of Hamlet, or the romantic picturesqueness of Claude Melnotte, he may well console himself with the reflection that few living actors have stimulated more the harmless enjoyment, honest pathos, and wholesome merriment of the public.

There is nothing malicious about the class of humour with which Mr. Toole is identified on or off the stage. The laughter which he evokes has no bitterness in it. Its ring is true as eighteen-carat gold, its source as honest as the day. In his most whimsical facial make-up there are many merry lines but no mean ones. The physiognomist would search in vain for danger-signals, but might discover plenty of indications of extravagant humour. With tears and laughter equally at his command, it is not surprising that Mr. Toole should be a prime favourite with audiences who appreciate above all else humour that is careful to keep "within the limits of becoming mirth," and when the inevitable day comes when the sock and buskin can no longer be donned by him, there will be tens of thousands who have enjoyed countless happy hours, thanks to his excellent talent, and who have learned to honour him alike as a man and an actor, to speak the kindly aspiration, "God rest his soul! He was a merry man!"

In his private life, too, if so well-known a public personage can fitly be said to have any private life, Mr. Toole has always been ready for a harmless joke, such as the little jest he played upon Mrs. Bancroft when, as Marie Wilton, a nervous slip of a girl, she was playing at the Lyceum in the same company as the comedian, and he made her, after many anxious inquiries as to the date and mysterious hints of something coming, a birthday present, wrapped up with infinite care in many thicknesses of silvery tissue paper, from which at last emerged—not a bracelet, as the youthful actress had hoped, but—a Tangerine orange! But Mr. Toole soon made up for the disappointment; and it was largely due to his encouraging and comical whisper to the timorous little actress at rehearsal, "Twenty pounds a week insisted upon, I think, after the first performance," that she found courage to fight her way bravely to the front.

To children Toole has always been particularly kind, and the gusto with which he tells the semi-pathetic, semi-humorous story of the little girl who played Tiny Tim, and apparently devoured an alarmingly large share of Bob Cratchit's Christmas goose—upon which, as a fact, the members of the family feasted each night right royally—proves how big a heart he has, and how tenderly susceptible it is to the claims and needs of childhood.

Mr. Toole, who is a thorough Londoner even when upon the stage, was born in St. Mary Axe, on March 12th, 1832, and speedily showed signs of possessing that mimetic faculty which is essential to comic acting of the best school. He was only twenty when, after a brief provincial apprenticeship, (having made his first appearance on the regular stage in Ipswich,—the birthplace of Mrs. Keeley,—as Sylvester Daggerwood, appearing, moreover, not as J. L. Toole but as John Lavers, a detail which is significant as proving that he had not then finally decided upon the stage as a career) he made his first appearance before a Metropolitan audience on July 22nd, 1852, upon the stage of the Haymarket Theatre, in a part which he first played at the Queen's Theatre, Dublin, and has played since times out of number, with unvarying success—that of Simmons, in *The Spitalfields Weaver*, in which *rôle* his whimsical humour and distinct individuality of style were quickly recognised as full of promise.

On October 2nd, 1854, Mr. Toole played the part of Sam Pepys, in *The King's Rival*, by Tom Taylor and Charles Reade, at the St. James's Theatre, appearing the same evening in a farce by Charles Selby, *My Friend the Major*, impersonating a sheriff's officer who is in a gentleman's house ostensibly as a friend, and has some comical experiences at a ball, with a jovial humour which speedily made its mark. During the same engagement Mr. Toole played Pierre, in *Honour before Titles*, with success.

From 1856 until 1859 Mr. Toole was a member of the Lyceum company, playing during his engagement such parts as Fanfaronade in *Belphegor* and Autolycus, in William Brough's amusing burlesque, *Perdita; or, The Royal Milkmaid*, and also gaining considerable favour by his vivacious and original acting as the hero of a farce called *Doing the Hansom*.

In 1859 Mr. Toole migrated to the new Adelphi Theatre under Benjamin Webster's management, and during his engagement had opportunities of displaying his talent in impersonating the heroes of eccentric comedy and farce, of which he eagerly availed himself. It was during this engagement that Mr. Toole created among other distinctly original and striking parts that of Asmodeus in the burlesque of that name, and Mr. Spriggins, in the still popular farce, *Ici on parle Français*—a character which has perhaps been the cause of more hearty laughter than any other in the actor's

MR. TOOLE AS CALEB PLUMMER.

répertoire; Augustus de Rosherville, the eccentric hero of *The Willow Copse;* and Wapshot in *The Life of an Actress;* while he gave proof of an almost Robsonian genius for blending homely humour with simple pathos in the parts of Bob Cratchit in *The Christmas Carol* and Caleb Plummer in *The Cricket on the Hearth.* In both of these characters Mr. Toole entered into the spirit of Dickens's delightfully tender and lovably humorous creations with a thoroughness and a delicacy of style which stamped him as an actor of the first degree of merit in his own school, capable of manifesting, when occasion arose, a simple pathos which went straight from heart to heart, and formed an indissoluble link of the pleasantest sort between the actor and his audience. Mr. Toole's Bob Cratchit and Caleb Plummer were, and are, an education in the art of painting the pathos and humour of humble life with a kindly and faithful touch, and the intense, real, living humanity of both characters won for the comedian immediate and enduring favour.

During the same year Mr. Toole created the part of William Kite in Watts Phillips' *Paper*

Wings, and appeared at Drury Lane as Enoch Flicker in a drama by the same author, called *A Story of* '45, transforming a comparatively insignificant part into *the* attraction, *par excellence*, of a successful play. In 1864 the comedian added to his reputation by his rendition of the principal character in Messrs. Brough and Halliday's lively farce, *The Area Belle*, in which he introduced that extraordinary effusion, "A Norrible Tale," which quickly took the taste of the town, and was sung, decades later, by Mr. Toole, into the receiving cylinder of a phonograph, the actor remarking afterwards to a friend, "How will that do?" an epilogue faithfully stored up by the instrument, to be reproduced in due course, although quite unintentionally added to the ditty.

In the following August Mr. Toole played the amusing part of Mr. Lysimachus Tootles in a comical piece called *My Wife's Maid*, and, a few weeks subsequently, created the part of Stephen Digges, in a piece of that name adapted for him specially by John Oxenford, from Balzac's famous novel, "Le Père Goriot," and affording the popular comedian ample scope for displaying in the one part both his humour and his pathetic power. The development of the character was effected with masterly art, and confirmed the judgment of those who saw in Mr. Toole the most likely successor to the mantle of Robson.

On January 30th, 1865, Mr. Toole appeared successfully as Fathom in an Adelphi revival of *The Hunchback*, and in the following July he created the *rôle* of Joe Bright, a plucky, straightforward fireman, in Mr. Walter Gadin's play, *Through Fire and Water*, with enormous skill, shining equally in the happier scenes and in the realistic episode of drunkenness.

In May 1866 Mr. Toole took the part of Prudent in *The Fast Family*, by Benjamin Webster, jun., adapted from Sardou's "La Famille Benoiton;" and in January 1886 he created the powerful part of Michael Garner, at the New Queen's Theatre, in Byron's comedy, *Dearer than Life*. Those who are familiar with Mr. Toole's method will quickly understand how entirely such a part enabled him to show his art at its best. The honourable, worthy, self-respecting tradesman, the affectionate husband and father stripping himself not only of his savings but of the good name which he values so highly, in order to save his son from shame, and then the pathetic pretence of high spirits when his misery was well-nigh breaking his heart,—all were represented by the actor with convincing force, and once again Mr. Toole proved that it was in the depicture of familiar experiences, with comedy and tragedy treading on each other's heels so closely as well-nigh to trip each other up, that he was to be seen at his best. It is well that we should be reminded now and again of the mirth and misery that are to be found in the most humdrum round of every-day life, and Mr. Toole in this and similar parts has brought this condition of existence to the surface in a conspicuously successful fashion.

Like Mr. Irving, who was also in the cast of this production, Mr. Toole has always been fond of going out into the highways and byeways of city and country, recognising odd bits of character with keen appreciation, and storing them up for future reproduction. The comedian, in particular, has always been peculiarly fond of studying human nature with all its unconscious elements of comedy and tragedy, obscure and humble as they might be, and it is a sterling proof of his genuine kindness of heart that he has always taken care that any one upon whom he played one of the harmless practical jokes so dear to his humour-loving soul, or who had afforded him some material for future use, was never left quite unrewarded. Even when sending presents to ailing friends Mr. Toole's kind thoughtfulness for others prompted him to habitually "put in a few trifles that might be useful to the landlady." Without doubt many a struggling soul has been lightened and brightened by the actor's kind-hearted consideration.

Mr. Toole's genuine good-nature has necessarily won him an unusually large number of friends, as distinguished from mere acquaintances, who have rejoiced with him in his happiness and success, and sympathised sincerely with him in the heavy sorrows which have fallen upon him from time to time in the death of those dearer to him than life.

Whether in the old days at Haverstock Hill,

in the little house with the garden where Robson would visit him on Sunday mornings and be cheered by the sight of his young friend pottering happily about amongst his plants; or in the pretty, cheerful house in Orme Square, facing Kensington Gardens, with its windows and balconies bright with flowers, "as who should say 'cheerfulness and fun are as the air we breathe,'" or later still, after the death of his well-loved son, in the cosy little house at No. 17, William Street, Lowndes Square, a stone's-throw from Charles Reade's "Naboth's Vineyard" at Albert Gate, with its busts of Shakespeare and Macready, its quaint old model of the "Maypole Inn," so dear to honest Gabriel Varden and his cronies, its countless souvenirs and tributes of affection and admiration from other artists, including a dainty, tender Thames study by Joseph Jefferson, the immortal "Rip," books, statuettes, relics of Charles Dickens, and general artistic litter of interesting and beautiful things, Mr. Toole's private life has always been the same—hospitable, honest, kindly, and that of a man whose home was, after all, his chief happiness.

At the Queen's Theatre, in July 1868, Mr. Toole impersonated Bob Acres with artistic moderation and in a spirit of true comedy, and in the following year he played Jack Snipe in Watts Phillips' drama, *Not Guilty*, and on December 13th, 1869, at the Gaiety Theatre in Byron's *Uncle Dick's Darling*, a play specially written for him, he created the part of Dick Dolland with unqualified success. It would not be easy to surpass the cleverness of the antithetic phases of the character—so jovial and full of spirits, and then so tender and so heartbroken. The affectionate devotion contrasted with the good-hearted geniality was dramatically effective to a degree, and Dick Dolland proved one of those literal transcripts of human nature which those who run may read, while the most critical students of original and copy could not detect any discrepancy worthy of note.

Mr. Toole followed up this success with a lengthened tour in the provinces, where he has always been an immense favourite, from the early days when the stage carpenter at Sheffield good-naturedly gave him the "wheeze" which he has since used with such effect in *The Steeplechase*, "It does make me so wild!"—a phrase introduced by a predecessor in the part, and given to Mr. Toole as a friendly, and, as it proved, really valuable hint.

In November 1871 Mr. Toole made his reappearance on the London stage as Paul Pry, at the Gaiety Theatre, bringing out all the quaint, dry humour of the part with excellent art, and appearing also in *The Spitalfields Weaver*, as Simmons, one of his earliest successes. On Boxing Day of the same year, and at the same theatre, he appeared as Thespis, in Mr. Gilbert's seasonable fantasy, called *Thespis; or, The Gods Grown Old;* and in April 1872, still at the Gaiety, he created the part of Neefit, in *Shilly-Shally*, by Anthony Trollope and Charles Reade; and in December 1873 appeared as Maw-worm in a revival of *The Hypocrite*, a comically lugubrious bit of acting in which he was seen to considerable advantage.

As Hammond Cooke, in Albery's comedy, *Wig and Gown*, Mr. Toole gave a clever, if rather extravagant, sketch of a barrister, in April 1874, at the Globe Theatre, painting

MR. TOOLE AS PAUL PRY.

with rare humour the shifts and struggles of a briefless barrister, full of petty pride, who really lives by letting furnished lodgings. In 1875 he went to America, and made an extended tour with complete success.

Before his departure for America Mr. Toole was the guest of the evening at a banquet held in Willis's Rooms, on Midsummer Day 1874, under the pleasant presidency of Lord Rosebery, who even then was an excellent after-dinner speaker. Lord Rosebery must surely have unconsciously possessed the gift of prophecy on that occasion when he said of Mr. Toole, "I should like to see a series of banquets given day after day in his honour until we had exhausted all the phases of his character. Still, although that might redound to his immortal glory, I am doubtful whether it would not result in his precipitate death from indigestion." This aspiration—as regards the banquets day by day, not, happily, the premature decease from dyspepsia—was almost literally fulfilled prior to the comedian's departure for Australia, nearly sixteen years later, where Mr. Toole found so many claims upon his time off the stage that he was often up night after night until four in the morning, withstanding the double strain with remarkable physical strength for a man of his years.

Upon the same occasion Lord Rosebery characterised Mr. Toole's humour rather curiously, as of a kind "grateful alike to age and to youth and to childhood—to the genius and to the fool"; and, a little later, an American critic emphasised this opinion by saying, with truth, that the test which Mr. Toole met was that, under all conditions of circumstance which arouse the best emotions of average humanity, his art made him the perfect reflection of the nature of mankind. "The colour was English but the fact was universal."

In December 1875 Mr. Toole created with great success the character of Mr. Tottle, in Byron's farcical comedy, *Tottle's*, at the Gaiety Theatre. The absurd incongruities of the wealthy quondam proprietor of Tottle's refreshment rooms, Tottle's eating house, Bucklersbury, and Tottle's *à la mode* beef shop, Borough Road, proving irresistibly funny, especially in the final act, when, half beside himself with jealousy, he plays fantastic tricks in the disguise of a waiter. Of course no such waiter could exist for five minutes in actuality without detection and expulsion, but the public do not ask Mr. Toole for realism. He is the Cruikshank, the Gavarni, the Pellegrini of the stage ; and naturalism, at all events in his purely comic assumptions, would be a disappointment to those who know and like him best.

It was at the Gaiety Theatre, too, in February 1877, that Mr. Toole created the part of Mr. Spicer Rumford in Mr. Burnand's extravagantly funny play, *Artful Cards;* and his comic bewilderment and dismay when discovered at the house of the doubtful Countess Asteriski, when the police make a raid upon it as a gambling-hell, his attempts to master the mysteries of " Bolo," and his forlorn appearance in Piccadilly, in the small hours of the morning, with battered hat, trombone, and ill-fitting ulster, were humorous pictures which remain in the memory.

In the same month Mr. Toole appeared at the Gaiety Theatre as Jacques Strop, in *Robert Macaire*, indulging in the most grotesque and fantastic business, and depicting the miserable rascal's comic despair and abject terror with exceptional vigour. The part became quite a new creation, and a remarkable one, in Mr. Toole's hands, and the humour, though wildly extravagant, was sufficiently possible to be intensely amusing.

January of 1878 saw Mr. Toole in a new part at the Globe Theatre, where he appeared as Chawles, or Charles Liquorpond, in Byron's *A Fool and his Money*, a scheming and grotesque butler, and an even more fantastic landowner in Wales, bothered comically enough with the language and customs of the Principality—a part which Mr. Toole made very entertaining in his own way.

The Folly Theatre, which cynical people promptly dubbed "Toole's Folly," in King William Street, Strand, was opened by Mr. Toole on November 17th, 1879, with a revival of *A Fool and his Money*, and in the new theatre Chawles proved a complete success. Mr. Toole's quaint gestures and sublime assumption of self-satisfaction took the taste of the town at once, and never has the unctuous imperturbability of a quondam autocrat of the servants' hall been more humorously portrayed.

On February 23rd, 1880, at a Covent Garden *matinée* revival of *Pickwick*, for the benefit of Mr. F. B. Chatterton, Mr. Toole gave his inimitably funny impersonation of Serjeant Buzfuz; and on March 31st he created the humorous character of Mr. Barnaby Doublechick, in Byron's comedy, *The Upper Crust*, a part in which, as the wealthy proprietor of Doublechick's Diaphanous Soap, he overflowed with humour and human nature. Mr. Toole apparently has a peculiarly shrewd insight into the idiosyncrasies of the successful trader class and their little weaknesses, and revels in the oddity of their characters, although not infrequently lapsing into caricature. On May 21st, 1881, Mr. Toole appeared as Cecil Strutton, Esq., in *Wits and Rabbits*, a one-act dramatic absurdity by Robert Reece and Knight Summers; in June *Artful Cards* was revived; and on July 20th he appeared as Mr. Norton Folgate in *Over the Garden Wall*, a one-act farce by Mr. Sydney Grundy.

On November 2nd, 1880, Mr. Toole created

with success the amusing *rôle* of Mr. Samuel Slithery, in a farce called *The Light Fantastic*, by Henry J. Byron.

Mr. Toole appeared as Mr. Bunny in *Auntie*, on March 13th, 1882, and on the re-opening of the theatre on October 7th, reappeared as Barnaby Doublechick, and also as Mr Guffin in *Guffin's Elopement*, by Messrs. Arthur Law and George Grossmith; singing a quaintly humorous song, "The Speaker's Eye," with his usual extravagant comicality; and on October 31st created the part of Solomon Protheroe, the cobbler-schoolmaster, in Mr. Pinero's play, *Girls and Boys*, a character which in less creative hands would probably have proved rather colourless and barren.

Always successful in caricature, towards which his professional habit seemed to have a natural bent, Mr. Toole was seen to great advantage as Loris Ipanoff Atiloff, Commander of the Reserve Forces, in *Stage Dora : or, Who killed Cock Robin?* a travestie *of Fédora*, by Mr. Burnand, produced at Toole's Theatre on May 26th, 1883, in which the comedian parodied the make-up, voice, and style of Mr. Coghlan with singular accuracy of perception and indisputable humour; and on February 14th, in the following year, he displayed an equal power of good-humoured travesty as Clawdian Andlivates, an "evergreen chappie," in Mr. Burnand's burlesque, *Paw Clawdian; or, The Roman Awry*, in which, as a classic masher, in toga, sandals, and white satin opera hat, and also in —it would scarcely be adequate to say with—a wonderful wax Roman nose as palpably false as any souvenir of Epsom Races, he was exceptionally funny. Though the nose was the nose of Barrett, the legs were the legs of Toole, and Mr. Toole's Clawdian possessed the humour of a caricature by "Ape." Between these successful parodies he had created the part of Kerosine Tredgold, in Mr. Law's farcical comedy, *A Mint of Money;* but neither the play nor the character proved to possess any striking novelty of conception, and Mr. Toole was funny in his own way, and that was all.

On December 6th, 1886, Mr. Toole created the part of David Trott, in Mr. and Mrs. Herman Merivale's domestic comedy, *The*

Butler, his dry humour enabling him to make a good deal out of a quaintly conceived and clearly delineated character of the kind in which he is seen to great advantage. At Miss Amy Roselle's benefit at the Lyceum on June 16th, 1887, Mr. Toole gave his capital impersonation of Spriggins in *Ici on parle Français*.

It is not difficult to understand that with such a part as Mr. Millikin, M.A., in Mr. and Mrs. Herman Merivale's *The Don*, produced on March 7th, 1888, Mr. Toole would display infinite humour, blended with a genial simplicity as irresistible as it was cleverly assumed. Mr. Millikin's inflammability as regards the fair sex was the *motif* of much amusing acting, and the part became one of the comedian's drollest and best. The play was revived on December 26th, after Mr. Toole's provincial tour, with renewed success, running again until the close of the season of 1889, on July 6th.

Before going to Australia on February 15th, 1890, Mr. Toole was the subject of well-nigh innumerable banquets, suppers, and genial gatherings expressive of goodwill. He was also the recipient of many good wishes from friends in all classes of society, as became—not only a man who had breakfasted with Mr. Gladstone and Professor Blackie, to the accompaniment of such an elevated tone of conversation that, on leaving Downing Street, the comedian was compelled to "talk to a policeman" in order to bring himself down to the level of ordinary life; but an actor who had expressed the opinion that "if the cultured people of a city were liberal in their patronage of the drama, nothing would tend more to elevate the stage, and improve the character of the pieces performed, compelling humourists to be wholesome and pure in their fun, and the more serious dramatists to be equally true in their pathos."

Upon the very eve of his departure, namely, on Friday, February 14th, 1890, the Prince of Wales gave a farewell dinner to Mr. Toole at the Garrick Club, amongst those present, besides the host and the principal guest, being the Duke of Fife, Lord Randolph Churchill, Lord Brooke, Sir Henry Thompson, Sir J. E. Boehm, Sir Charles Russell, Dr. Russell, Mr. F. C. Burnand, Mr. Edward Lawson, Mr.

G. A. Sala, and Mr. George Lewis. Mr. Toole subsequently went to supper at the Beefsteak Club-room at the Lyceum Theatre. He left Charing Cross on Saturday morning at 11 o'clock, Mr. Clement Scott accompanying him during the earlier part of his journey, and bidding him a final " God-speed!"

www.ingramcontent.com/pod-product-compliance
Lightning Source LLC
Chambersburg PA
CBHW020223240426
43672CB00006B/402